AIA Guide
to St. Paul's
Summit Avenue
and Hill District

Publication of the

AIA Guide to St. Paul's Summit Avenue and

Hill District has been made possible

through generous gifts from

A Society of The American Institute of Architects

John R. Camp

George A. MacPherson Fund

Elmer L. and Eleanor Andersen Fund

Bean Family Fund for Business History

North Star Fund of the Minnesota Historical Society

Larry Millett

AIA Guide to St. Paul's Summit Avenue and Hill District

Minnesota Historical Society Press

www.mhspress.org

The Minnesota Historical Society Press is a member of the Association of American University Presses.

10 9 8 7 6 5 4 3 2 1

International Standard Book Number
ISBN 13: 978-0-87351-644-0 (paper)
ISBN 10: 0-87351-644-3 (paper)

Library of Congress Cataloging-in-Publication Data
Millett, Larry, 1947–
    AIA guide to St. Paul's Summit Avenue and Hill District /
Larry Millett.
        p.   cm.
    Includes bibliographical references and index.
    ISBN-13: 978-0-87351-644-0
    ISBN-10: 0-87351-644-3
  1. Architecture—Minnesota—Saint Paul—Guidebooks.
  2. Saint Paul (Minn.)—Buildings, structures, etc.—Guidebooks.
  3. Saint Paul (Minn.)—Guidebooks.
  I. Title.

NA735.S24M55   2009
720.9776'581—dc22

                                        2008050844

Front cover: James J. Hill House detail, 365 Summit Avenue detail, Cathedral of St. Paul, Mount Zion Temple detail, William Lightner House detail, all by Bill Jolitz

Back cover: Portland Avenue cupola, Blair House detail, *Indian Hunter* statue, all by Bill Jolitz

Cover design: Cathy Spengler Design

Contents

Symbols Used in this Guidebook

! A building or place of exceptional architectural and/or historical significance

N Individually listed on the National Register of Historic Places or included within a National Register Historic District

L Locally designated as a historic property or within a local historic district

Abbreviations Used for Select Architectural Firms

ESG Architects   Elness, Swenson Graham Architects

HGA   Hammel, Green and Abrahamson

Author's Note: This book is a revised, updated, and slightly expanded version of the chapter devoted to Summit Avenue and the Hill District in my *AIA Guide to the Twin Cities*, published in 2007. Some entries here appear exactly as they are in that book; others have been changed to reflect new information or to provide additional historic background. I have also included a number of entries for buildings that either were omitted from the *AIA Guide* because of space limitations or have been built since its publication.

Locator map: St. Paul's Summit Avenue and Hill District

Map Area Enlarged

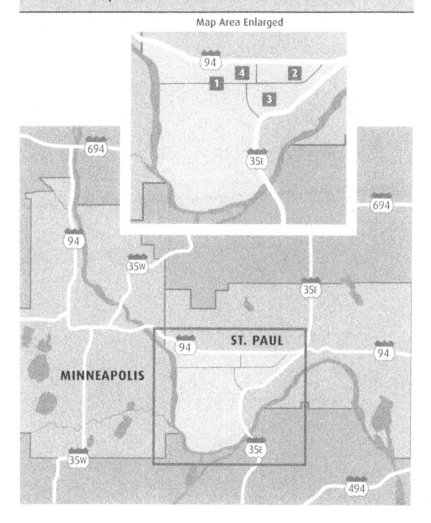

1 Summit Avenue
2 Ramsey Hill
3 Summit Hill
4 Summit-University West and North

AIA Guide to St. Paul's Summit Avenue and Hill District

Overview

Summit Avenue and the Hill District occupy the geographic and historic heart of St. Paul. It was here that F. Scott Fitzgerald began his
dreamy, melancholic life in the chilly shadows of wealth and privi-
lege and here too that the city's greatest builders—Archbishop John
Ireland and James J. Hill—left behind mighty monuments for the
ages. Fitzgerald once famously remarked that there are "no second
acts in American lives," but the same could not be said of the Hill District, which fell into decay over many decades before a new generation
of urban pioneers touched off a remarkable renaissance beginning in
the late 1960s. With many of its Victorian-era homes and buildings
now beautifully restored, the neighborhood today looks as elegant
and well kept as it ever has.

At the center of it all is Summit Avenue, St. Paul's most renowned
street, a midwestern mansion row that extends for nearly five miles
through the western half of the city, finally terminating at the Mississippi River. St. Paul's leading architects—including Cass Gilbert,
Clarence Johnston, and Allen Stem—designed fine homes here, and
today the entire avenue is protected within national and local historic
districts. The Burbank-Livingston-Griggs House (1863), the James J.
Hill House (1891), Gilbert's superb Lightner House (1893), and Johnston's Dittenhofer House (1908) are among the avenue's architectural
treasures.

Summit also serves literally as ground zero for much of its course,
since it's the dividing line between north and south street addresses in
St. Paul. It plays an equally essential role in what might be called the
city's sense of self. St. Paulites take great pride in the avenue, and its
very name conjures up images of huge houses, monumental churches,
wide green lawns, and a refined and gracious way of life.

Although best known for its mansions, Summit is also home to
some of St. Paul's most notable churches, beginning with the gigantic
St. Paul Cathedral (1915). Other fine churches along Summit include
St. Paul's on the Hill (1913), House of Hope Presbyterian (1914), and St.
Thomas More (formerly St. Luke's), completed in 1925. Mount Zion
Temple (1955), designed by Erich Mendelsohn, is the avenue's out-
standing work of modern architecture.

The Hill District, which extends north and south of Summit, has
gone by quite a few names over the years, creating the sort of con-
fusing, ad-hoc nomenclature for which St. Paul is all too renowned.
Ramsey Hill, Summit Hill, and Summit-University are the officially designated neighborhoods here, but names such as Crocus Hill, Cathedral
Hill, St. Anthony Hill, Rondo, and Selby-Dale still have their adherents.
Whatever you choose to call it, the Hill District, which was added to
the National Register of Historic Places in 1976, is an extraordinary
residential environment. Extending back from the high bluffs overlooking downtown, the district is one of the nation's great repositories
of late Victorian-era housing, most of it designed by prominent local
architects.

The district consists of two distinct neighborhoods. North of Summit is Ramsey Hill, much of which is in a local historic district as well
as the larger National Register district. Victorian houses of every size,
shape, and style populate the streets of Ramsey Hill, which includes
the lower—and most spectacular—stretch of Summit Avenue. Summit
is indeed the big attraction here, but if you wander along the side
streets you'll discover numerous architectural gems, ranging from the
stone-walled Luckert House (1858) to the lovely little Virginia Street
Church (1887) to Laurel Terrace (1887), the city's most magnificent
row house.

Officially, Ramsey Hill is part of the larger neighborhood known as Summit-University, which runs north to University Avenue and west to Lexington. The heart of St. Paul's black community is in this neighborhood, although many residents were uprooted in the 1960s by construction of Interstate 94, which obliterated historic Rondo Avenue as well as many homes and buildings.

South of Summit and extending along the bluffs to Lexington Parkway is Summit Hill, popularly known as Crocus Hill. This is a gold-plated residential precinct, its long blocks lined with large, well-maintained houses. Some of the most desirable homes here cling to the blufftops, where a tangle of short streets, loops, and cul-de-sacs creates the sense of a private enclave. For visitors, Summit Hill's biggest attraction is Grand Avenue, which has evolved into St. Paul's favorite upscale shopping district. Running parallel to and a block south of Summit, Grand offers an eclectic mix of homes, apartments, restaurants, and retail businesses, all of which manage to coexist in relative harmony (although parking issues remain eternally nettlesome).

The history of Summit Avenue and the Hill District goes back to the earliest days of the city. The first mansions appeared on the crest of Summit by the 1850s, when settlers also began building homes farther out along nearby streets. Only a handful of these first-generation dwellings survive, among them the much modified Stuart-Driscoll House (1858 and later), the oldest home on Summit. The rest of the Hill District didn't begin to fill in until after the Civil War, but even then development was hampered by a lack of ready transportation to the downtown area.

The district began its most rapid period of growth in the 1880s, abetted by the provision of city water service in 1884 and the completion of a cable car line along Selby Avenue in 1887. Three years later, St. Paul's first electrified streetcars began operating on Grand. With its high elevation, proximity to downtown, and relatively level terrain suitable for home building, the Hill District became *the* place to live in St. Paul. The district had one other significant advantage, which was that it was well away from the noisy, smoky, and smelly railroad lines that made most other near-downtown neighborhoods less than ideal residential quarters. Development came a bit later to much of the Summit Hill area, in part because of its distance from the Selby cable car line, but once trolleys began running on Grand, Summit Hill also saw new home construction that continued well into the early decades of the twentieth century.

Much of the Hill District, and to a lesser extent Summit Avenue, began a long slide into decrepitude in the 1930s. Old mansions became down-at-the-heels rooming houses or were subdivided into numerous apartments. In other cases, homes stood vacant for years. Even so, the district's stock of historic properties remained more or less intact, in part because of geography: the bluffs separating the Hill District from downtown St. Paul formed a natural barrier against commercial sprawl. St. Paul's less than dynamic economy also minimized development pressure.

In the late 1960s and early 1970s, a great turnaround began in the Hill District. Young couples discovered the neighborhood's long-neglected Victorian homes, which could be bought for the proverbial song, and began restoring them. Neighborhood associations and non-profit developers like Old Town Restorations, Inc., spurred preservation efforts and also built new infill housing in cooperation with an alphabet soup of city, state, and federal agencies. Today, just as in the nineteenth century, the Hill District is one of St. Paul's most desirable places to live.

1 Summit Avenue

Summit Avenue

Summit Avenue's most distinguished historian, Ernest Sandeen, pronounced it "the best preserved American example of the Victorian monumental residential boulevard," and it is hard to dispute that judgment. Mansion-lined boulevards, from Park Avenue in Minneapolis to Prairie Avenue in Chicago to Euclid Avenue in Cleveland, could once be found in many American cities, but Summit alone has managed to come down through the years with its historic housing stock relatively intact.

Impressive as they are, Summit's mansions have inspired strong criticism from a few notable naysayers. F. Scott Fitzgerald, who lived for a time on Summit, called it "a museum of American architectural failures." Frank Lloyd Wright, with his usual dismissive aplomb, labeled the avenue "the worst collection of architecture in the entire world." Neither comment is true, but it is fair to say that only a handful of Summit's mansions rank among the best American houses of their time. Most, in fact, are similar to mansions found in other large cities across the United States.

Yet, as Sandeen understood so well, what counts on Summit is less the individual excellence of its homes than its totality as a preserved environment. In his book *St. Paul's Historic Summit Avenue,* first published in 1978, Sandeen calculated that of the 440 houses built on Summit up to that time, 373 survived—a truly remarkable number. A scattering of new homes and condominiums has appeared along the avenue since 1978, but little if anything has come down, making the survival rate even more impressive.

Summit is also exceptional by virtue of the fact that it has always been fully integrated into the life of St. Paul. Wealth in most places tends to hide away behind walls, gates, hedges, and even armed guards. By contrast, Summit's big houses, posing forthrightly behind their broad lawns, are there for all to see and enjoy. Because of this, most St. Paulites view Summit not as an exclusive enclave of the rich but as a four-and-a-half-mile-long public promenade with some wonderful architectural scenery. So it is and so, one hopes, it always will be.

Summit Avenue Map 1

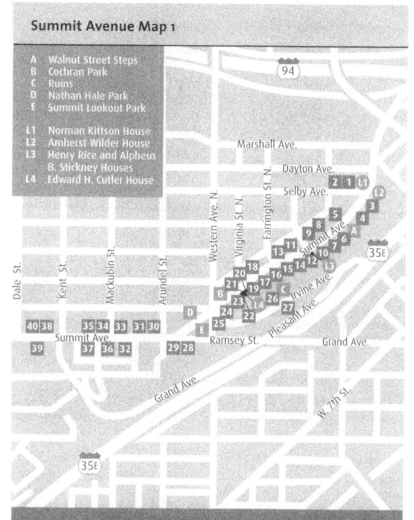

A   Walnut Street Steps
B   Cochran Park
C   Ruins
D   Nathan Hale Park
E   Summit Lookout Park

L1   Norman Kittson House
L2   Amherst Wilder House
L3   Henry Rice and Alpheus
     B. Stickney Houses
L4   Edward H. Cutler House

1 Cathedral of St. Paul	20 College of Visual Arts
2 Sacristy	21 Condominiums
3 Archdiocese Chancery and	22 House
Residence	23 Egil and Rachel Boeckman House
4 James J. Hill House	24 Summit Bluff Townhouses
5 Horace P. Rugg House	25 Irvine Avenue
6 Louis and Maud Hill House	26 House
7 Driscoll-Weyerhaeuser House	27 House
8 Joshua Sanders House	28 University Club
9 Summit Manor Reception House	29 Burbank-Livingston-Griggs House
10 Condominiums	30 Shipman-Greve House
11 Frederick A. Fogg House	31 William and Bertha Constans House
12 George Lindsay House	32 Chauncey and Martha Griggs
13 Germanic-American	House & 490 Summit
Institute Haus	33 Cyrus B. Thurston House
14 Stuart-Driscoll House	34 George W. Freeman House
15 William Lightner House	35 W. W. Bishop House
16 William Lightner–George Young	36 William Butler House
Double House	37 Walter J. S. Traill–Homer Clark House
17 Edgar Long House	38 Summit Terrace
18 Crawford Livingston House	39 Greve and Lillian Oppenheim House
19 Thomas and Clare Scott House	40 Double house

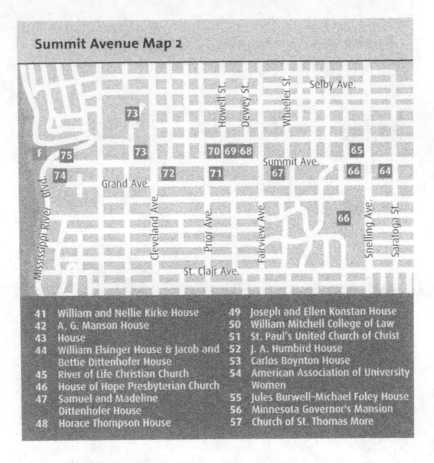

Summit Avenue Map 2

41   William and Nellie Kirke House
42   A. G. Manson House
43   House
44   William Elsinger House & Jacob and
      Bettie Dittenhofer House
45   River of Life Christian Church
46   House of Hope Presbyterian Church
47   Samuel and Madeline
      Dittenhofer House
48   Horace Thompson House
49   Joseph and Ellen Konstan House
50   William Mitchell College of Law
51   St. Paul's United Church of Christ
52   J. A. Humbird House
53   Carlos Boynton House
54   American Association of University
      Women
55   Jules Burwell-Michael Foley House
56   Minnesota Governor's Mansion
57   Church of St. Thomas More

1 Cathedral of St. Paul ! N L

201 Summit Ave. (also 239
Selby Ave.)

*Emmanuel Masqueray, 1915 /
interior, Maginnis and Walsh
(Boston), 1925–31 / renovation,
Foster Dunwiddie Architects,
2003 / Notable art: altar canopy,
Whitney Warren, 1924 / "Te
Deum" and "Magnificat" (bronze
grilles), Albert H. Atkins, 1926 /
"The Resurrection," "The Beati-
tudes," and "The Jesuit Martyrs"
(stained-glass rose windows),
Charles Connick, 1932, 1940*

It's possible to think of St. Paul
without this vast church of gray
granite, but just barely. From its
incomparable site on St. Anthony
Hill, the cathedral is—along with
the nearby State Capitol—one of
the city's defining monuments,
its dome visible from almost
every corner of St. Paul. Summit
Ave. itself had to be moved 90
feet to the south to make room
for the cathedral, which does

nothing on a small scale.

Despite its grandeur, the
cathedral has been criticized
as something like the SUV of
churches, too large and top-
heavy for its own good. F. Scott
Fitzgerald, for example, likened
it to "a big white bulldog on its
haunches," and he wasn't being
complimentary. The cathedral
does convey a sense of aggressive
purpose, and its muscular architecture seems as much an expres-
sion of power as it is of faith.
Step inside, however, and whatever doubts you may have are
overwhelmed by the cathedral's
mighty reality. *Awe* is a word sel-
dom used in architectural dis-
course anymore, but it certainly
applies here. The sweep of space
beneath the dome simply has no
equal in the Twin Cities.

This cathedral is actually
St. Paul's fourth; the first three,
beginning with the log chapel
built by Father Lucien Galtier in
1841, were all located downtown

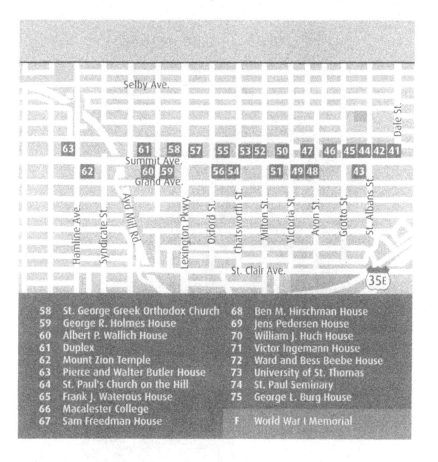

and are now gone. It owes its existence to a pair of extraordinary men: Archbishop John Ireland, who presided over the St. Paul–Minneapolis Archdiocese from 1888 to 1918, and French-born architect Emmanuel Masqueray, who trained at the prestigious École des Beaux-Arts in Paris before moving to the United States in the 1880s. Ireland was visiting the Louisiana Purchase Exposition (better known as the St. Louis World's Fair) in May 1904 when he was introduced to Masqueray, the fair's chief designer. The two connected at once. Less than a year later, Masqueray moved to St. Paul and began to design the cathedral.

Following a symmetrical Greek cross plan, the cathedral mixes Renaissance and Baroque Revival elements in a way very much Masqueray's own. As a result, the church is anything but "pure" in its style or its proportions, and the 306-foot-high dome has always seemed like a giant head on a body not quite large enough to support it. Among the cathedral's most distinctive elements are three huge "telephone dial" rose windows—a Masqueray trademark.

Although the cathedral was dedicated in 1915 after eight years of construction, its interior of whitewashed brick was still quite stark. Another 25 years were required to substantially complete it. Masqueray died in 1917, Ireland a year later, and in 1923 the Boston firm of Maginnis and Walsh was called in to take charge of the project and also to design two new buildings—a rectory and sacristy—at the rear of the cathedral.

Inside the cathedral, finishing work proceeded through the 1930s. The brick walls were clad with Mankato-Kasota limestone over a base of French marble while artists (at least 17 in all) provided such embellishments as stained-

Cathedral of St. Paul

glass windows and a rich variety of sculpture. Among the outstanding artworks is a monumental baldachin, or altar canopy, designed by New York architect Whitney Warren (for whom Masqueray once worked). Equally impressive are the bronze grilles by Albert H. Atkins installed between the sanctuary and the ambulatory and the huge rose windows designed by Charles Connick. The interior was largely complete by 1940 except for decoration of the inner dome, which wasn't undertaken until the 1950s.

Beginning in 2001, the cathedral's exterior was repaired and restored at a cost of $32 million (about 20 times the original construction price). Workers sheathed the dome and roof in 100,000 square feet of new copper, cleaned and tuckpointed the Rockville granite facades, repaired windows, and upgraded mechanical and electrical systems. The project was finished in 2003, and the cathedral now looks as mighty and magnificent as it ever has, although more than a few St. Paulites miss the old copper dome's green patina, which is unlikely to reappear because air pollution just isn't what it used to be.

Cathedral interior

Free tours of the cathedral, available on Mondays, Wednesdays, and Fridays at 1 PM, offer an opportunity to learn more about this grandest of all Twin Cities churches.

2 Sacristy N L

Maginnis and Walsh, 1925 / Art: angel (sculpture atop dome), Ernest Pellegrini, 1925

An elegant building that complements the cathedral while managing to make a small statement of its own. Linked to the rear of the cathedral, the sacristy is in the form of a domed octagon, faced entirely in Briar Hill stone from Ohio. Atop the copper-clad dome, an angel sculpted by New

Sacristy angel

York artist Ernest Pellegrini poses in prayer. The rectory next door at 239 Selby Ave., also designed by Maginnis and Walsh, dates to 1924.

Norman Kittson House, 1888

LOST 1 *Before the cathedral was built, its site was occupied by the* **Norman Kittson House,** *a towered French Second Empire mansion. Built for a millionaire business- man and designed by pioneer St. Paul architect Abraham Radcliffe, the mansion was completed in 1884. Kittson didn't enjoy it for long; he died onboard a train to Chicago in 1888. After his death, the mansion devolved into a less than first-class boardinghouse. Agents for Archbishop Ireland bought the property for $52,000 in 1904, and the mansion was razed a year later.*

3 Archdiocese Chancery and Residence N *L*

226–30 Summit Ave.

Cerny and Associates, 1963

A nicely crafted complex that displays the highly formal, clas- sically inspired brand of mod- ernism popular in the 1960s. Unfortunately, the one-story chancery is out of sync with the historic two- and three-story homes on this part of the avenue.

Amherst Wilder House, 1895

LOST 2 *Among Summit Ave.'s more than 60 lost mansions, the largest and finest was the* **Amherst Wilder House,** *located where the chancery now stands. Designed by architects William Willcox and Clarence Johnston, it was built in 1887. Wilder, whose fortune contin- ues to finance good works in St. Paul, lived in the house until his death in 1894. Like the James J. Hill House, the Wilder mansion was later owned by the St. Paul– Minneapolis Archdiocese. Instead of being preserved, however, it was torn down in 1959—a great loss to the city.*

4 James J. Hill House ! N *L*

240 Summit Ave.

Peabody, Stearns and Furber (Boston), Irving and Casson (Boston), James Brodie, 1891

A stone hunk of a house that per- fectly expresses the power and strength of its original owner, who roared through life like a locomotive but who also believed in building things to last. Hill's first St. Paul mansion, constructed in 1878, was a standard French Second Empire affair in Lower- town. By the mid-1880s, however, Lowertown was no longer an

James J. Hill House

attractive residential district and Summit Ave. had become the place to be.

Hill selected the Boston firm of Peabody, Stearns and Furber as his architects. They designed a mansion of reddish Massachusetts sandstone that is still St. Paul's largest home, with 36,000 square feet spread over five floors. Stylistically, the mansion is an example of the bulked-up Romanesque Revival style pioneered by H. H. Richardson. The project didn't proceed smoothly. Hill battled the architects, who in 1889 decided they could override his orders regarding some stonework. Big mistake. He promptly fired them and hired another firm. His in-house architect, James Brodie, also helped see the house through to completion.

The mansion seems rather forbidding, in part because its lively reddish brown walls were

Hill House interior

blackened over the years by coal smoke (the restored porte cochere shows the stone's original color). While *warmth* and *charm* aren't words you'd use to

describe the mansion, it's actually quite inviting inside. If you wander into the dining room or library in particular, you'll find gorgeously carved woodwork, executed by German-born craftsman John Kirchmayer. The house also has a lovely skylit art gallery, while to the rear are a series of open porches that provide views across the city.

Hill died in the house in 1916 and left no will even though his fortune has been estimated at about 20 billion in today's dollars. His wife, Mary, stayed in the house until her death in 1921, after which four of Hill's daughters donated the house to the St. Paul–Minneapolis Archdiocese, which used it for more than 50 years. The Minnesota Historical Society acquired the mansion in 1978; it's now a house museum open for tours and other events.

POI A Walnut Street Steps

Between Summit and Irvine Aves.

ca. 1901

Walnut was once a platted street here, officially 66 feet wide, though the terrain was so steep that the right-of-way could accommodate foot traffic only by means of a stairway. When James J. Hill's son Louis decided in 1901 to build a house next door, Hill petitioned to vacate the street. Hill got his wish, but not before

Summit Avenue

the city required him to build a new staircase on the old right-of-way that would be forever open to the public. The stairs, bordered by a massive sandstone wall, remain in use today.

Horace P. Rugg House

5 Horace P. Rugg House N *L*

251 Summit Ave.

Hodgson and Stem, 1887

One of the most original and sophisticated designs on Summit. Mixing Romanesque and Renaissance Revival elements, the house is so tall and narrow that it has the feel of a commercial building. Its brickwork is also intriguing: rising above a sandstone base, the long Roman bricks are arranged in alternating bands of color that gradually dissolve into a single field as they reach the third floor. The house is entered through a porch embellished with much stone carving. Note in particular the six caryatids, all in different poses, although music making appears to be their principal activity. Built for a Lowertown wholesaler who dealt in pumps and plumbing supplies, the house is now subdivided into condominiums.

6 Louis and Maud Hill House N *L*

260 Summit Ave.

Clarence H. Johnston, 1903 / front addition, Charles S. Frost, 1913 / restored, Close Associates (Gar Hargens), 2004–5

This might be called the *other* Hill House, and it's certainly impressive in its own right, not to mention the only home in St. Paul ever to host the queen of Romania (in 1926). Louis Hill, James J. Hill's second son, commissioned the house just before his marriage to Maud Van Courtland Taylor in 1901. An 1850s house was cleared before work began on the mansion, a serene red

Louis and Maud Hill House

brick Georgian Revival house set well back on the lot to capture views from the blufftop. In 1913 a large addition was placed across the front of the house, obscuring the 1903 facade (although the original front portico was reinstalled). The addition included four guest rooms and a second-floor ballroom. Later, a swimming pool was added in the basement. After Louis Hill's death in 1948, the house was purchased by a Roman Catholic educational guild, which in 1961 sold it to the Daughters of the Heart of Mary for use as a Catholic retreat center. Rechristened "Dove Hill" by its present owners, the house has been beautifully restored and now functions once again as a single-family home.

Driscoll-Weyerhaeuser House

7 Driscoll-Weyerhaeuser House N *L*

266 Summit Ave.

William H. Willcox, 1884

An early Queen Anne house with many of the usual bells and whistles—a slender round tower, decorative chimneys, and lots of busy brick- and stonework. Its first owner, Frederick Driscoll, was general manager of the *St. Paul Pioneer Press.* In 1900 the house was purchased by lumber baron Frederick Weyerhaeuser. He soon established friendly relations with his near neighbor, James J. Hill, who conveniently owned large tracts of western timberland. Deals were struck, and they must have been good ones, for Weyerhaeuser ultimately became even richer than Hill. The house's classical entry porch is not original, nor is the porte cochere, which was added in the 1990s.

Joshua Sanders House

8 Joshua Sanders House N *L*

271 Summit Ave.

George Wirth, 1882

A late Italianate house with a central tower and a woodworker's dream of a front porch. It is now condominiums.

9 Summit Manor Reception (Charles Schuneman) House N *L*

275 Summit Ave.

Clarence H. Johnston, 1901

One of a number of broad stone houses, medieval in character, built on Summit and elsewhere in the Hill District around 1900. The house was originally owned by Charles Schuneman, partner in a department store bearing the family name located at Sixth and Wabasha Sts. in downtown St. Paul. The store survived until 1958, when it was merged into Dayton's.

10 Condominiums N *L*

280 Summit Ave.

1996

A modern attempt at Renaissance Revival, rendered not very impressively in stucco.

Frederick A. Fogg House

11 Frederick A. Fogg House N *L*

285 Summit Ave.

Allen H. Stem, 1899

Another fascinating design from Allen Stem. The basic style is Colonial Revival, but it's treated here in an unusually monumental fashion. Note the distinctive first- and second-story transoms over the windows and the elegant way in which the front door's sidelights merge into a double arch above. The half-moon windows beneath the eaves illuminate what was once a ballroom. Frederick Fogg was a director of the St. Paul Fire and Marine Insurance Co. (now Travelers) and later served as superintendent of Ramsey County schools. Stem, incidentally, designed a very similar house for R. L. Wright at 30 Crocus Pl.

*LOST 3 Two mansions of note—the **Henry Rice House** and the **Alpheus B. Stickney House**—were once located at 288 Summit Ave. The Rice House, built in 1855 for a pioneer businessman and politician, was one of the first homes on Summit. It was torn down in 1884 to make way for a huge stone mansion for Stickney, an organizer of the Union Stockyards in South St. Paul. After Stickney's death in 1916, the mansion stood vacant for 14 years before being demolished.*

12 George Lindsay House N *L*

294 Summit Ave.

Parker Thomas and Rice (Boston), 1919 / later addition

A straightforward, if extremely large, example of Colonial Revival. It's the only wood-clad house on the bluff side of Summit, an anomaly that may be explained by the fact that Lindsay was an associate of timber titan Frederick Weyerhaeuser. Among the later owners of the house, in fact, was one of Weyerhaeuser's grandsons.

Germanic-American Institute Haus

13 Germanic-American Institute Haus (George W. Gardner House) N *L*

301 Summit Ave.

Thomas Holyoke, 1905

Holyoke, who worked as Cass Gilbert's chief draftsman before striking out on his own, designed five houses on Summit around the turn of the century. This Georgian Revival was built for George W. Gardner, who made his money in real estate and insurance. The house has been owned since 1965 by the Volksfest Association, a German cultural organization.

14 Stuart-Driscoll House N *L*

312 Summit Ave.

1858 / additions, 1910, 1918

Summit's oldest house, an Italian Villa–style mansion with much Classical Revival updating. Built for lumber dealer David Stuart, the house originally sported a cupola and a balustraded front terrace. Among later owners was Herman Haupt, a West Point–

trained engineer who served as a brigadier general in the Civil War and later became the Pennsylvania Railroad's chief engineer.

Stuart-Driscoll House

In 1881 Haupt moved to St. Paul to become general manager of the Northern Pacific Railroad. The house's three-story rear addition was built in 1918 by Arthur Driscoll, who owned the property from 1901 to 1949

15 William Lightner House ! N *L*

318 Summit Ave.

Cass Gilbert, 1893 / renovated and restored, Thomas Blanck, 2006

Cass Gilbert at the top of his form, and one of Summit's greatest houses. It's the last and best of a trio of Gilbert-designed mansions that form a row along the avenue's bluff side. At a time when Richardsonian Romanesque was already giving way to Classical Revival, Gilbert here combined the two into one compact yet monumental package. The sandstone arch around the front door is a Richardsonian trademark, as are the squat columns with Byzantine-inspired capitals that screen a row of inset windows above. But the rest of the front facade, built of rough-faced blocks of South Dakota quartzite, has the symmetry and calm lines of classically inspired architecture. The house was built for William Lightner, a lawyer who just seven years earlier had commissioned Gilbert and his then partner, James Knox Taylor, to design the double house next door. Once

William Lightner House

subdivided into seven apartments, the house was restored in 2006 to a single-family home.

William Lightner–George Young Double House (left) & Edgar Long House

16 William Lightner–George Young Double House N *L*

322–24 Summit Ave.

Gilbert and Taylor, 1888 / renovated, JLG Architects, 2006

Although undeniably imposing, this double house—now three condominiums—isn't as crisp and masterful as the Lightner house next door. The western half has a formal, Renaissance Revival character; the eastern side tends more toward the informalities of the Queen Anne and even has a shingled side gable. Arched stone porches add a Romanesque Revival note to the proceedings. William Lightner built this house with his law partner, George Young.

17 Edgar Long House N *L*

332 Summit Ave.

Gilbert and Taylor, 1889

A broad, towered, brick and stone house in the general realm of Romanesque Revival. The tower and central gable display fine floral carvings. Within the open front porch, small stained-glass windows line up beside arched double entry doors. The bricked-in wing above the tuck-under garage was originally an open porte cochere. Edgar Long was in the railroad and building construction businesses and may have met Gilbert because their offices were in the same downtown building. Below the house, on Irvine Ave., are some interesting ruins.

18 Crawford Livingston House N *L*

339 Summit Ave.

Cass Gilbert, 1898

Another of Gilbert's exercises in what might be called picturesque symmetry. Here, the arcaded loggia evokes the Venetian Renaissance while the central dormer far above strikes a medieval pose with its steeply pitched roof and Gothic bargeboards. These romantic elements are reined in by strict overall symmetry, however,

Crawford Livingston House

and the result is a house that seems to be having some—but not too much—fun. Now divided into five condominiums, the house was originally owned by Crawford Livingston, Jr., whose business interests included utilities and railroads.

Thomas and Clare Scott House

19 Thomas and Clare Scott House N *L*

340 Summit Ave.

Allen H. Stem (Reed and Stem), 1894

One of St. Paul's largest residential versions of a Renaissance palace, turned on its side to accommodate the lot and entered via a long side porch. Thomas Scott was a banker and insurance executive. The house was later owned by George Thompson, president of the Pioneer Press and Dispatch Printing Co., and then by Samuel and Charlotte Shepard, who in the 1920s redid much of the interior with materials and furnishings imported from Europe. The house was renovated by new owners in 2005.

20 College of Visual Arts (Watson P. Davidson House) N *L*

344 Summit Ave.

Thomas Holyoke, 1915

The details are Tudor Revival, but the near-perfect symmetry of the facade is Beaux-Arts. The original owner was president of a prominent St. Paul real estate firm. The College of Visual Arts has occupied the house since 1961.

21 Condominiums N *L*

362–64 Summit Ave.

1977

The neighbors didn't much care for these flat-roofed condominiums, the first new homes built on this section of Summit since the 1950s. The placement of the garages in front is indeed unfortunate. At least the architects didn't try to fake it by giving the homes a nostalgic appliqué—almost always a bad strategy in historic districts.

22 House (carriage house) N *L*

Rear of 362–64 Summit Ave.

ca 1875 / renovated, Joseph Michaels, 1968

Once part of the Edward H. Cutler estate, this is one of many carriage houses in the Hill District that have been turned into stylish housing.

LOST 4 *The condominiums at 362–64 Summit occupy the site of the **Edward H. Cutler House,** built in 1875 in the prevailing Italianate style and enlarged and remodeled in the 1880s. It was razed in 1968— one of the last demolitions to occur on the blufftop portion of Summit.*

23 Egil and Rachel Boeckman House N *L*

366 Summit Ave.

David Adler and Robert Work (Chicago), 1928

In the early 1920s a Shingle Style house that had occupied this site for 40 years was torn down. Dr. Egil Boeckman and his wife,

Rachel (a daughter of James J. Hill), acquired the property and built a new house in the fashion-

Egil and Rachel Boeckman House

able Georgian Revival mode. A hefty split pediment over the front door is one of many impressive details.

POI B Cochran Park N L

Summit and Western Aves.

1924 / shelter, Holyoke and Jemne (Edwin Lundie), 1926 / Art: The Indian Hunter (statue), Paul Manship, 1927

A delightful little park on a triangle of land donated to the city by Emilie Cochran in memory of her husband, Thomas, an investment banker who, among other things, once arranged a $500,000 loan for an aspiring Minneapolis retailer named George Dayton. The site had been an informal children's playground before the park was built. Architect Edwin Lundie, who designed the stone shelter, is best known for his exquisite Period Revival homes and north woods cottages. Paul Manship, a St. Paul native, was a leading sculptor of the art deco era and called the statue here one of his favorites. His best-known work is a gilded *Prometheus* at Rockefeller Center in New York City.

24 Summit Bluff Townhouses N L

376–78 Summit Ave.

Bentz/Thompson/Rietow Architects, 1982, 1986

A textbook example of sensitive infill design, these shingle-clad townhouses—by far the best of

Summit's modern-era housing—feature a series of layered front gables sharply outlined by white trim. The gables call to mind the

Summit Bluff Townhouses

avenue's traditional architecture but in an abstracted way that is unmistakably modern. Later infill housing on the avenue has generally opted for a more literal-minded, and far less successful, sort of historicism.

25 Irvine Avenue

Bluffs below Summit Ave. from near Ramsey St. to Walnut St. steps

This alleylike street plunges downhill here before dividing into two levels as it clings to the steep face of the bluffs below Summit. Old carriage houses (some renovated), newer homes, and even a ruin or two can be found along Irvine, which in the summer when the foliage is lush has the feel of a secret world all but unknown to the city around it.

26 House N L

333 Irvine Ave.

Kadoch Design, 2004

A four-level house built with poured concrete walls and clad in cultured stone. It works well on this site.

POI C Ruins

Irvine Ave. beneath 332 Summit Ave.

About the closest thing to an Old World ruin in the Twin Cities. These picturesque stone remains were once a large carriage house on the Edgar Long estate.

Carriage house ruins

27 House

314 Irvine Ave.

1996

A neo–Arts and Crafts on Irvine's lower level.

POI D Nathan Hale Park N *L*

Summit and Portland Aves., ca. 1900

Art: Nathan Hale *(statue), William Partridge, 1907*

The Revolutionary War patriot whose only regret was that he had too few lives to give for his country is memorialized here.

Summit Lookout Park

POI E Summit Lookout Park N *L*

Summit Ave. and Ramsey St.

ca. 1887 / Art: New York Life Eagle *(bronze sculpture), Augustus and Louis St. Gaudens, ca. 1889*

This small park with sweeping views of the city was from the 1860s until the 1880s home to a hotel known as Carpenter's Lookout. Today, its chief occupant is a bronze eagle sculpted by brothers Augustus and Louis St. Gaudens

and originally mounted over the entrance of the New York Life Building (1889–1967) downtown. Public Art St. Paul led the effort to relocate the eagle, which was restored at a cost of almost $100,000 and installed here in 2004. Some critics think the eagle is facing the wrong way—it looks back toward Summit rather than out across the river valley—but regardless of its orientation it qualifies as one of the city's most impressive pieces of public art. The park's other outstanding feature is a huge retaining wall along the Ramsey St. hill built of Mankato-Kasota limestone. Dating to the late nineteenth century, the wall was restored by the City of St. Paul in the 1990s.

University Club

28 University Club N *L*

420 Summit Ave.

Reed and Stem, 1913

A gracious Tudor Revival club building. The dining room is open to the public and offers some of the best views in the city. Formed in 1904 as the St. Paul Club by wealthy young men from the neighborhood, the name was changed in 1910 when a new rule required members to be attending college at the time they joined.

29 Burbank-Livingston-Griggs House ! N *L*

432 Summit Ave.

Otis Wheelock (Chicago), 1863 / remodeled, Clarence H. Johnston, 1884, 1895 / addition, Allen H. Stem, 1925 / interior remodeled, Magnus Jemne, 1930, Edwin Lundie, 1930–33

This romantic limestone pile is the finest surviving mansion of

Burbank-Livingston-Griggs House

its era in the Twin Cities. It's also a museum of local design, its richly detailed interior worked and reworked over the years by some of St. Paul's leading architects. The home's builder was James C. Burbank, a Vermonter who migrated to St. Paul in 1850 and made a fortune by establishing a fleet of packet boats and operating stagecoach lines. In 1863, when Summit was little more than a dusty carriage trail, he spent $22,000 (a phenomenal sum in those days) to erect this country estate. The house is a primer in the high-style Italianate of the 1860s. Its irregular massing, deep bracketed cornices with pendants, and tall arched windows framed by voussoirs all convey a sense of the picturesque, as does the cupola crowned by an ornate finial.

After Burbank's death, a succession of owners hired prominent St. Paul architects to enlarge, renovate, and redecorate the house. In 1884 Clarence Johnston created a magnificent new front stair hall and inserted a triple-arched window to the right of the front door for short-term owner George Finch. Eleven years later, Johnston updated the house's porches in the latest neoclassical style. In 1925 Allen Stem—working for the home's then owner, Crawford Livingston—designed a two-story addition to the rear. Livingston's daughter, Mary, and

her husband, Theodore Griggs, acquired the property in 1925 and hired Magnus Jemne and then Edwin Lundie to undertake a series of interior renovations in various period styles. The house was donated to the Minnesota Historical Society in 1967 but proved too costly to maintain. In 1996 the house was sold to the University Club next door and is now used as a residence.

Shipman-Greve House

30 Shipman-Greve House N L

445 Summit Ave.

LeRoy Buffington, 1882, 1884 / addition, ca. 1920s

This may be St. Paul's first Queen Anne–style house, and it remains one of the best, beautifully crafted in stone, wood, brick, and stucco. Although it shows an array of influences—the porch, for example, has a distinctly Chinese feel—the house is much more restrained than the rambling, towered, gingerbread-laden extravaganzas usually classified as Queen Anne. Instead, it evokes the quietly picturesque, Tudor-tinged work of English Arts and Crafts architects like Richard Norman Shaw. The 1876 Centennial Exposition in Philadelphia, which included two Shavian houses built for British delegates, helped popularize the style in this country. Six years later, architect LeRoy Buffington brought the style to St. Paul with this house, commissioned for an obscure businessman, Henry Shipman, who decamped to warmer climes in 1883 after selling the uncompleted home to Herman Greve, a real estate broker. A west-side addition was constructed in the 1920s, but otherwise the house has survived largely intact.

that the house acquired its most curious element—an oblong projection at the peak of the roof that has been likened to a coffin because of its shape and the swags that create the appearance of handles. So far as is known, however, no funeral is pending.

Chauncey and Martha Griggs House (left) & 490 Summit

William and Bertha Constans House

31 William and Bertha Constans House N L

465 Summit Ave.

Augustus Gauger, 1886 / remodeled, ca. 1920s, ca. 1969

The portion of Summit east of Snelling Ave. saw a huge building boom in the early 1880s, when over 40 mansions were built. This house was designed for William Constans, who arrived from France in 1850 and whose business enterprises included a wholesale brewery supply firm out of which the Schmidt Brewing Co. evolved. In its original form, the house had a five-story tower at its southeastern corner and a Queen Anne–style front porch. A subsequent owner, Walter Hill (one of James J.'s sons), gave the house an extensive Georgian Revival makeover in the 1920s by removing the tower, replacing the old porch with one more classical in character, and adding new molding and other decorative details. It was during this time

32 Chauncey and Martha Griggs House N L

476 Summit Ave.

Clarence H. Johnston, 1885

490 Summit (Addison G. Foster House) N L

490 Summit Ave.

Clarence H. Johnston, 1884

These complementary mansions were designed for business partners by Clarence Johnston in the first year of his practice. The Foster House—now used for weddings, receptions, and other events—is an energetic assembly of pieces that don't quite add up to a convincing whole. The Griggs House is a better design, more disciplined and monumental than its neighbor. It's also one of the first homes in St. Paul to be built of Lake Superior sandstone. Unfortunately, a large attic skylight added in 1939, when the house was being used as an art school, tends to undercut Johnston's overall design. Chauncey Griggs and Addison Foster were partners in a lumber and coal business. Both moved to Tacoma, WA, in about 1887 and continued, very successfully, in business there. Foster later served one term as a U.S. senator. Incidentally, the Griggs House is said to be haunted by at least five ghosts, which must make for some exciting Halloween parties.

Cyrus B. Thurston House

33 Cyrus B. Thurston House N *L*

495 Summit Ave.

1881

A very appealing Victorian, nicely restored. Like many other large houses built in the Twin Cities around 1880, it's moving toward Eastlake and Queen Anne but can't shake off such Italianate vestiges as window hoods and eaves brackets. The tall, narrow windows also evoke the Italianate. Note the home's date in a panel above the side gable overlooking Mackubin St. Cyrus Thurston was a dealer in carriages and also operated a cold-storage warehouse near downtown's Seven Corners. The house was later owned by Dr. Rudolph Schiffman, whose coat of arms (with the initials *R. S.*) can be found above the front porch.

34 George W. Freeman House N *L*

505 Summit Ave.

Cass Gilbert, 1896

Another of Gilbert's Gothic-tinged houses that combines medieval motifs with rigorous symmetry. George Freeman, president of the Conrad Gotzian Shoe Co., was well acquainted with Gilbert's work before commissioning this house: the architect had already designed two buildings in Lowertown for the firm.

35 W. W. Bishop House N *L*

513 Summit Ave.

Wirth and Haas, 1887

One of the few wood-frame Queen Anne houses on this part of Summit. It has a polygonal tower and an elaborate front gable that seems to be Flemish in inspiration. W. W. Bishop was a real estate agent about whom little is known. The property later became a boardinghouse, whose

W. W. Bishop House

residents around 1920 included Donald Ogden Stewart, the screenwriter of such classic films as *Dinner at Eight* (1933) and *The Prisoner of Zenda* (1937).

36 William Butler House N *L*

516 Summit Ave.

Butler Brothers Construction Co., 1914

A Renaissance Revival house with an unusual color palette that includes yellow brick, gray granite trim, and a green tile roof. The small terrace overlooking Summit is a graceful touch in a design that otherwise seems curiously mechanical, especially in the arrangement of the windows. The house was built for William Butler, who with four of his brothers owned a prominent St. Paul construction company that built the State Capitol, among many other projects. Another of the Butler brothers, Pierce, later served as U.S. Supreme Court justice. In 1917–18 the house was leased to Sinclair Lewis, who came to St. Paul to work on a book about James J. Hill. The book was never completed, but in 1920 Lewis published *Main Street*, the novel that made him famous.

37 Walter J. S. Traill–Homer Clark House N *L*

534 Summit Ave.

Abraham M. Radcliffe, 1884 / remodeled, ca. 1920s? / renovated, ca. 2000 and later

This home's dramatic roof sweeps down to form a rampart arch sheltering a porte cochere. The house as it appears today is largely the result of an extensive remodeling in the 1920s as well

Walter J. S. Traill–Homer Clark House

as more recent renovation work. Walter J. S. Traill was a grain dealer who began his career in Canada as a clerk for the Hudson's Bay Co. Homer Clark, president of West Publishing Co. in the 1920s, later owned the house and was responsible for its Tudor Revival makeover.

38 Summit Terrace N *L*

587–601 Summit Ave.

Willcox and Johnston, 1889

A brownstone row house that leaves no Victorian style unaccounted for, although the general flavor is Romanesque Revival. Johnston, minus Willcox, also designed the much tamer row house at 596–604 Summit, completed in 1890. Architecture does not explain why Summit Terrace is a National Historic Landmark, however: its notoriety derives from its association with F. Scott Fitzgerald. The writer's parents, Edward and Mollie, moved into one of the row house's eight units, at 593 Summit, in 1914 when Fitzgerald was a student at Princeton University. In 1918 they relocated to the unit at 599 Summit, and it was here in July and August 1919 that Fitzgerald, often working around the clock in a

third-story room, rewrote the manuscript that became his first novel. Accepted by Scribner's in mid-September, just days before Fitzgerald's 23rd birthday, and published in 1920, *This Side of Paradise* sold 50,000 copies and propelled its author to instant fame.

Greve and Lillian Oppenheim House

39 Greve and Lillian Oppenheim House N *L*

590 Summit Ave.

Ellerbe and Round, 1913

One of two notable Prairie Style houses on Summit, not up to the standards of Frank Lloyd Wright but competently done. The French doors in the projecting front bay are unusual for a home of this kind. Franklin Ellerbe and Olin Round designed one other Prairie Style building of note—a bank in Mankato, MN, that also dates to 1913. Greve Oppenheim was a real estate investor and the son of Ansel Oppenheim, a lawyer whose house at 275 Summit burned down in 1895.

40 Double house N *L*

603–5 Summit Ave.

1987

This double house touched off a brouhaha when it was built

Summit Terrace

because its pink-tinted stucco was considered far too gaudy by Summit's guardians of good taste. It is now boringly neutral in color.

William and Nellie Kirke House

41 William and Nellie Kirke House N L

629 Summit Ave.

Clarence H. Johnston, 1896

A collision between a small French chateau and something out of merry old England. Among the noteworthy details is a pair of exquisite front doors. William Kirke was in the insurance and real estate businesses. In April 1910, a few days before his 51st birthday, he "fell dead on Dale Street" (as one newspaper starkly put it) while walking toward Grand Ave. to catch a streetcar.

42 A. G. Manson House N L

649 Summit Ave.

1874

This French Second Empire house earned a permanent place in the lore of Summit Ave. when John Kessler and Thomas Maguire acquired it in 1919 with the intention of opening a funeral parlor. Corpse-averse neighbors fought the plan, and the St. Paul City Council soon passed an ordinance forbidding funeral homes in residential neighborhoods. Undaunted, Kessler and Maguire opened their mortuary and were promptly arrested for this, ah, grave offense. The case went to the Minnesota Supreme Court, which sided with the city and thereby preserved Summit for the living.

43 House N L

696 Summit Ave.

Alladin Improvement Co., 1963

Modern infill at its most unfathomably stupid. This small house was inserted here as someone's idea of a suitable addition to Summit Ave. Blame it on the bad karma of the 1960s.

William Elsinger (right) & Jacob and Bettie Dittenhofer Houses

44 William Elsinger House N L

701 Summit Ave.

Clarence H. Johnston, 1898

Jacob and Bettie Dittenhofer House N L

705 Summit Ave.

Cass Gilbert, 1898 / remodeled, Clarence H. Johnston, 1913

These houses form one of the most intriguing duos on Summit. Built in the same year and designed by St. Paul's two leading architects, both are constructed of Mankato-Kasota stone, feature Medieval-inspired details, and are basically foursquare in form. Yet their effects are quite different. Gilbert, ever the classicist, gave the Dittenhofer House a symmetrical front facade that has a decided Beaux-Arts heft to it. Johnston—though moving in a classical direction—clung to a more picturesque Victorian manner, evident in the Elsinger House's corner tower and the off-center bay and dormer above the porch.

As with other decisively paired houses on Summit, these were built for families who knew each other well. William Elsinger and Jacob Dittenhofer were partners in the Golden Rule Department Store in downtown St. Paul. They were also brothers-in law: Bettie

House of Hope Presbyterian Church

Dittenhofer was Elsinger's sister. In 1913 Johnston was called upon to remodel the Dittenhofer house, no doubt because Gilbert was by that time a very busy architect in New York City, having just overseen completion of his Woolworth Building, then the world's tallest skyscraper.

45 River of Life Christian Church (First Church of Christ Scientist) N L

739 Summit Ave.

Clarence H. Johnston, 1913 / remodeled, 1947, 1951, and later

A monumental brick church in the Roman classical mode, more simply detailed than typical Beaux-Arts productions of the era. Within, four corner staircases lead up to a second-floor auditorium originally illuminated by skylights (removed in 1951). The River of Life Church has occupied the building since 1996.

46 House of Hope Presbyterian Church N L

797 Summit Ave.

Cram, Goodhue and Ferguson (Boston), 1914 / addition, Harold E. Wagner, 1959 / Art: stained-glass windows, Charles Connick and others

A very correct if not especially scintillating Gothic Revival church, which with its attendant buildings forms perhaps the most sophisticated example of this style in St. Paul. The original portions of the

complex were designed by the firm of Ralph Adams Cram, a leading American church architect whose work includes such monuments as the Cathedral of St. John the Divine in New York City.

Here, Cram chose his favored late English Gothic style, setting a steeply roofed nave in front of a square, pinnacled bell tower. Exterior detailing is quite chaste in keeping with Cram's desire to achieve a quiet effect. The surprisingly intimate sanctuary features floor tiles from Pewabic Pottery of Detroit, a timber-beamed ceiling, and stained-glass windows designed by a number of artists, including Charles Connick, whose work also graces the St. Paul Cathedral. To the east of the main church is an education wing added in 1959. A chapel, offices, library, and other rooms are also incorporated into the church complex, which surrounds an inner courtyard known as a garth.

House of Hope is among the oldest Protestant congregations in St. Paul, founded in 1855. Its first permanent church, completed in 1873, was located downtown on a site just north of where RiverCentre now stands. The congregation decided to merge with the First Presbyterian Church in 1907 and then began laying plans for this church. Over the years, House of Hope has been the congregation of choice for many of St. Paul's most prominent families.

Samuel and Madeline Dittenhofer House

47 Samuel and Madeline Dittenhofer House N L

807 Summit Ave.

Clarence H. Johnston, 1908, 1911

Clarence Johnston designed 38 houses on Summit, and this one is surely among his best. He could be a rather stodgy designer, but here he produced a bold, powerful, and very long (at 81 feet) house, distinguished by an enormous eastern gable that plunges down to the first floor. Positioned in the middle of the gable may well be the largest dormer on any house in the Twin Cities. Department store magnate Jacob Dittenhofer built the house as a wedding present for his son, Samuel, and his bride, Madeline Lang. The couple lived here until 1936, when they went off to Europe, where they found themselves trapped in Paris after the outbreak of World War II. Clearly preferring Europe to St. Paul, they never returned to the house, which stood vacant until Madeline donated it to the Christian Brothers in 1966 for use as a provincialate. The brothers sold the house in 1999, and it is now once again a single-family home.

48 Horace Thompson House N L

808 Summit Ave.

H. I. Wicks (Green and Wicks, Buffalo), 1903

A banker's palace, straight from the Italian Renaissance by way of

Horace Thompson House

Buffalo, NY (where the architects practiced). Compared to the over-ripe Beaux-Arts piles often built on the East Coast at this time, the Thompson House is commendably restrained, concentrating its ornamental energy on a columned porte cochere, a classical cornice, and a parapet wall with balusters. The house is now subdivided into two condominiums.

49 Joseph and Ellen Konstan House N L

828 Summit Ave

SALA Architects, 2002

An expensive attempt, done with considerable skill, to reproduce the "old look" of Summit in a new Colonial Revival house. Trouble is, this house and other recent nostalgic infills can't compete with the avenue's elaborately detailed historic homes on their own terms. What Summit really needs are high-quality infill houses showcasing the best of contemporary design as opposed to reiterations of the past.

50 William Mitchell College of Law N *L*

875 Summit Ave.

Ellerbe and Co., 1931 / addition, 1957 / addition (Warren E. Burger Library), Winsor/Faricy Architects, 1990 / addition, Perkins and Will (Chicago), 2005

The oldest part of this complex, along Portland Ave., is a handsome Romanesque Revival building from 1931 that was originally St. Luke's School and later became Our Lady of Peace Catholic High School for girls. William Mitchell, a law school whose roots go back over 100 years in the Twin Cities, bought the building in 1976 and has undertaken two expansions since then. The Warren E. Burger Library, which faces directly on Summit, is named after a William Mitchell graduate who served as chief justice of the U.S. Supreme Court from 1969 to 1986.

51 St. Paul's United Church of Christ N *L*

900 Summit Ave.

Ingemann and Bergstedt, 1952

A large version of the boxy churches that were popular in the early 1950s, modern in spirit but not aggressively so. A sculpture of Christ adorns the entrance on Summit.

52 J. A. Humbird House N *L*

937 Summit Ave.

Cass Gilbert, 1899

One of Gilbert's last St. Paul houses and a rather modest one at that. The house next door at 943 Summit was also designed by Gilbert and is said to have originally been identical to its neighbor. Local lore holds that the houses were for many years occupied by sisters who later got into a bitter quarrel, causing the owner of 943 Summit to alter her house so as to spite her sibling. The memorably named Humbird, who built both houses, was in the lumber business.

53 Carlos Boynton House N *L*

955 Summit Ave.

Clarence H. Johnston, 1904

A Tudor Revival house with baroque elements such as the semicircular pediment above one of the dormers. The ornament that dances all around the roof is some of the finest on Summit.

American Association of University Women

54 American Association of University Women (Henry and Ruth Allen House) N *L*

990 Summit Ave.

Thomas Holyoke, 1916 / addition, Harry Schroeder, 1966

An unusually rugged and rather somber Georgian Revival mansion, its walls laid up in random coursed blocks of rough-faced limestone. The house was built for Henry G. Allen, a wholesale grocer, and his wife, Ruth. The St. Paul branch of the American Association of University Women, which has owned the property since 1949, uses it as a clubhouse.

55 Jules Burwell–Michael Foley House N *L*

1003 Summit Ave.

Allen H. Stem, 1891 / remodeled, Clarence H. Johnston, 1906

This house as it appears today is largely the work of Clarence Johnston, who was hired by the second owner, Michael Foley, to redesign what had originally been a wood-frame, Colonial Revival home. Johnston faced the house in red sandstone, added bay windows on the second floor, and designed a superb wraparound porch that flares out gracefully over the front steps. The result is a strong design that achieves Beaux-Arts monumentality without entirely abandoning the home's Colonial Revival heritage.

56 Minnesota Governor's Mansion (Horace and Clotilde Irvine House) N L

1006 Summit Ave.

William Channing Whitney, 1912 / Art: Man-Nam (sculpture), Paul Granlund, 1970 (located in yard west of mansion)

A standard (albeit very large) Tudor Revival exercise in red brick and stone, designed by a Minneapolis architect who specialized in mansions for the moneyed class. It was built for lumberman Horace Irvine and his wife, Clotilde, both of whom lived in the house until their deaths. In 1965 their daughters donated the house to the state for use as a governor's mansion and guesthouse.

The house has a contentious history. Governor Rudy Perpich complained in the 1980s that the roof leaked and once led news reporters on a tour of the attic to show them the source of the trouble. Another colorful governor, Jesse Ventura, refused to live in the house after his election in 1998 and later shut down the mansion in a dispute with the state legislature over security costs. Despite these contretemps, the mansion—officially known as the Minnesota State Ceremonial Building—remains in use and is open for public tours.

Church of St. Thomas More

57 Church of St. Thomas More (St. Luke's Catholic Church) N L

1079 Summit Ave.

Comes Perry McMullen (Pittsburgh) with Slifer and Abrahamson, 1925

One of the city's outstanding parish churches, a free interpretation of French and Italian Romanesque rendered in smooth limestone. The Summit Ave. facade features elaborately carved portals, the largest of which depicts Christ and a variety of saints, conveniently identified in panels for those unschooled in hagiology. Above the main portal is a spectacular rose window set within a patterned frame. Farther up, dwarf columns form galleries to either side of a figure of St. Luke. Inside, the church has a kind of muscular simplicity. A coffered, barrel-vaulted ceiling rises over the long nave, which has arcaded side aisles mounted on thick columns. The church once had lavish mural work, but most of it was painted over in the 1980s.

Emmanuel Masqueray was the first choice for designing the

Minnesota Governor's Mansion

church; however, after his premature death in 1917 the project went to John T. Comes of Pittsburgh. Comes also died at a relatively young age, in 1922, and the church was finished by others, including Frederick Slifer and Frank Abrahamson, two of Masqueray's former draftsmen. All told, the church was under construction for nine years. A basement chapel, now called the lower church, was the first section to be completed, in 1919. The upper church took another seven years. A school, rectory, and convent, all built after the church, complete the parish campus. In 2008 the church's name was changed to St. Thomas More when another Catholic parish merged with St. Luke's.

58 St. George Greek Orthodox Church N L

1111 Summit Ave.

Voight-Fourre, 1967

A 1960s version of the Byzantine style, complete with a golden dome.

59 George R. Holmes House N L

1156 Summit Ave.

Charles Bassford, 1907

At first glance, this broad-fronted, foursquare house appears to be little different from quite a few others on the avenue. A closer look, however, reveals unusual baroque-inspired features such as the sculpted dormer pediments and the elongated column capitals (on both the porch and the second story) that project out from the entablature. All in all, a one-of-a-kind house for what was, in Bassford's case, a one-of-a-kind job, since he never designed another home on Summit.

60 Albert P. Wallich House N L

1164 Summit Ave.

Alden and Harris, 1914

A fine Craftsman house, crisply executed in dark brick with light cast-stone trim. Note the curving, elongated cruciform shape that decorates each of the front gateposts. This shape appears frequently in the work of the Chicago architect Louis Sullivan

Albert P. Wallich House

and can be found throughout his only building in Minnesota, the National Farmers Bank (1908) in Owatonna. The motif's highly visible placement here suggests an homage to Sullivan, whose buildings and writings inspired many of the era's progressive architects.

61 Duplex N L

1205 Summit Ave.

William F. Keefe, 1922

Windows with geometric patterns add a Prairie Style note to what is otherwise a duplex typical of the era.

62 Mount Zion Temple ! N L

1300 Summit Ave.

Erich Mendelsohn with Bergstedt and Hirsch, 1955 / renovated and restored, Bentz/Thompson/ Rietow Architects, 1997–2003

Home to St. Paul's oldest Jewish congregation, founded in 1856, this synagogue is the most striking modern-era building on Summit. It's also the last work of Erich Mendelsohn, a pioneer modernist who first gained attention for architectural sketches he produced while in the German army during World War I. In the 1920s he designed a series of remarkable department stores in Germany but moved to England and later Palestine after the Nazis came to power. He immigrated to the United States in 1941 and designed synagogues in St. Louis, Cleveland, and Grand Rapids (MI) before receiving the commission for Mount Zion in 1950. Mendelsohn died suddenly in 1953,

Mount Zion Temple

before the temple was finished, and St. Paul architect Milton Bergstedt completed the work.

Two boxlike, copper-clad volumes that house the sanctuary and a small chapel dominate the composition, rising dramatically above the main mass of the brick building, which includes a long education wing. These simple cubic forms were adopted after Mendelsohn's original design—featuring two tall volumes formed by bold triangular arches arranged in the manner of accordion pleats—proved too costly to build. Mendelsohn described the sanctuary and chapel, which have serenely elegant interiors, as "point and counterpoint," and they do indeed establish an intriguing architectural dialogue.

Mendelsohn's design isn't entirely successful. His decision to angle the temple away from the street grid makes for an awkward relationship with Summit, while changes in the design left the Hamline Ave. side of the building poorly resolved. After receiving a number of additions and alterations over the years, the temple was expertly renovated by Bentz/Thompson/ Rietow Architects between 1997 and 2003.

63 Pierce and Walter Butler House N L

1345–47 Summit Ave.

Clarence H. Johnston, 1895

With its picturesque stepped and curved gables, this brick double house is one of Summit's more exotic specimens of architectural

theater. It's done up in a late phase of the Tudor style sometimes called Jacobean Revival, inspired by English manor houses built during the seventeenth-century

Pierce and Walter Butler House

reign of King James I. Clarence Johnston rummaged through pretty much every style in the book during his long career designing mansions on Summit, and while this house may not be his finest, it's certainly among the most fun to look at. Walter Butler was a founder of the Butler Brothers contracting firm, which undertook projects—including railroad and automobile tunnels—across the United States. At the time this double house was built, his brother, Pierce, was the Ramsey County attorney. Pierce later went on to a lucrative career representing railroads. In 1922 he was appointed to the U.S. Supreme Court; he remained a justice until his death in 1939.

64 St. Paul's Church on the Hill N L

1524 Summit Ave.

Emmanuel Masqueray, 1913 / additions, 1922 and later

Although best known for his overpowering cathedral a few miles away, Emmanuel Masqueray also worked deftly on a smaller scale. This handsome limestone church, built for Minnesota's second-oldest Episcopal congregation, is

St. Paul's Church on the Hill

in the English Gothic Revival style that Masqueray preferred for Protestant churches. The copper-clad spire is especially fine. Within, you'll find an altar, woodwork, and stained glass, including two Tiffany windows, all salvaged from the congregation's long-vanished first church, built in 1858 in Lowertown.

65 Frank J. Waterous House N *L*

1591 Summit Ave.

Thomas Ivey (builder), 1904

Cute is not a word that comes readily to mind when describing the average home on Summit. But it's appropriate in the case of this property, built for the aptly named vice president of a family company that manufactured fire-fighting apparatus, including the first fire pump powered by a gasoline engine.

66 Macalester College

1600 Summit Ave.

Various architects, 1884 and later

Macalester was founded in 1874 as an outgrowth of two acade-mies established by the Reverend Edward Neill, a pioneer Presbyte-rian clergyman. It's named after one of Neill's wealthy friends, Philadelphia businessman Charles Macalester, who donated a build-ing for the college at its original location in Minneapolis. The col-lege moved here in 1885 after the completion of Old Main, the first

building on campus. Since then, the college has gradually added buildings in a wide variety of his-toric and modern styles. The lay-out of the campus does little to unite its eclectic architecture. The biggest problem is that busy Grand Ave. cuts through cam-pus—an arrangement approved in 1890 as part of a deal to extend streetcar service to the area.

Old Main, Macalester College

Old Main, a doughty Roman-esque Revival pile designed by Willcox and Johnston, still serves as the campus centerpiece. It was built in two stages, in 1884 and 1888. The older east wing was demolished in the 1980s to make way for a new library. The remain-ing part is home to the college's administrative offices. The other architectural highlight here is **Weyerhaeuser Memorial Chapel,** designed by Cerny and Associates in 1968. Set above a dry moat, the chapel is a glass-walled hexagon that encloses a warm but muscu-lar worship space supported by treelike columns.

67 Sam Freedman House N *L*

1774 Summit Ave.

1922

A modest house for Summit, mildly Tudor, although its pris-tine coat of white stucco and its calm lines evoke the English Arts and Crafts style.

68 Ben M. Hirschman House N *L*

1855 Summit Ave.

Ralph Mather, 1916

A good example of the Italian Renaissance Revival style popular with mansion builders in the early twentieth century. The entrance porch, with its carefully spaced columns, is particularly well done. Ben Hirschman was a partner in a wholesale liquor firm. In 1925 he sold the house to William McKnight, then the general manager and soon to be president of 3M.

Jens Pedersen House

69 Jens Pedersen House N L

1865 Summit Ave.

Jens Pedersen, 1922

A fine Craftsman house built for and by Jens Pedersen, who operated a house plan service in St. Paul for many years. Pedersen's grandson, William Pedersen of Kohn Pedersen Fox Architects in New York, designed the Travelers insurance headquarters building in downtown St. Paul.

70 William J. Huch House N L

1905 Summit Ave.

Scherer Co. (Los Angeles), 1928

The Spanish Colonial Revival style proved quite popular in the Twin Cities in the 1920s, perhaps because it encouraged fantasies of a place without winter. This house by a California architect shows off the style nicely and even comes with what may be the only walled *front* patio on Summit.

71 Victor Ingemann House N L

1936 Summit Ave.

Ingemann and Co., 1912

A Tudor Revival beauty notable for its intricate brickwork, which is laid up in a mason's holiday of patterns, including a broad herringbone band that wraps around the second story. The ornate bargeboards over the front porch, said to have been carved in Denmark, are also a delight. Although

its textures and forms are picturesque, the house as a whole is disciplined by a strict attention to symmetry.

Victor Ingemann House

The builder of this unusually well-detailed house was himself a contractor. Victor Ingemann and his brother, George, started their business in 1884 and went on to construct hundreds of houses and other buildings in the Twin Cities. Victor's son, William, became a prominent St. Paul architect.

Ward and Bess Beebe House

72 Ward and Bess Beebe House N L

2022 Summit Ave.

Purcell Feick and Elmslie, 1912

The only house in St. Paul by William Purcell and George Elmslie, the Minneapolis-based masters of the Prairie Style. Although the style is associated with the low spreading forms of Frank Lloyd Wright, Purcell and Elmslie designed a number of high-gabled houses such as this one that draw on elements from English Arts and Crafts architecture. Even so, the house's recessed entrance, banded windows, wide eaves, and open floor plan are all Prairie trademarks. This wasn't a big-budget house, so it lacks the art-glass windows often found in Purcell and Elmslie's work. However, there's a fretsawn ornament, in one of Elmslie's characteristically intricate patterns, adjoining the main entrance. The house, which cost $6,000, was built for Dr. Ward Beebe, a bacteriologist, and his wife, Bess, as a wedding present from her parents.

Quad, University of St. Thomas

73 University of St. Thomas

2115 Summit Ave.

Various architects, 1885 and later

The University of St. Thomas began as a combination seminary and college founded by Archbishop John Ireland in 1885. Today it's the state's largest private college, enrolling over 10,000 students. Its campus here (there's also one in downtown Minneapolis) sprawls across more than 14 square blocks, including parts of the St. Paul Seminary complex.

The oldest buildings occupy the northern part of the original campus. Here you'll find the university's most notable monument—the **Chapel of St. Thomas Aquinas** (121 Cleveland Ave. North), an elegant Renaissance-inspired church from 1918 designed by Emmanuel Masqueray, architect of the St. Paul Cathedral. The heart of the campus, immediately north of Summit, consists of a quadrangle of Collegiate Gothic buildings, all faced in golden Mankato-Kasota limestone. These buildings date to the 1930s and later.

Because of St. Thomas's steady growth, the campus seems to be perpetually expanding—long a sore point with neighbors. The university has already taken over much of the St. Paul Seminary campus and has also added new buildings on the south side of Summit, including **Owens Science Hall** (1997) and **McNeely**

Hall (2006), home to the business school. Both follow the university's standard Collegiate Gothic template, which has never produced much in the way of scintillating architecture. A new student center, scheduled to open in 2011 at the northeast corner of Summit and Cretin Aves., is the next big project in the works.

Residence hall, St. Paul Seminary

74 St. Paul Seminary

2260 Summit Ave.

Cass Gilbert, Clarence H. Johnston, Emmanuel Masqueray, and others, 1894 and later

Established in 1894 by Archbishop John Ireland, this seminary occupies expansive grounds along the east side of the Mississippi River gorge. Railroad titan James J. Hill donated $500,000 to build and endow the seminary, which was created to train diocesan priests. A man who liked to stay close to his money, Hill functioned something like the seminary's construction superintendent, weighing in on every detail. Cass Gilbert designed the first six

St. Mary's Chapel

campus buildings in a Renaissance Revival style that's as stiff as a Roman collar. Three of these original buildings, including **Loris and Cretin Residence Halls** (both 1894), still stand.

At least eight more buildings were added to the campus over the next century. By far the most significant of these is **St. Mary's Chapel** (1905), designed by Clarence Johnston and modeled on a Roman basilica from AD 380. Clad in rockfaced Kettle River sandstone with Indiana limestone trim, the chapel is small but exquisitely detailed, with carved stonework, a stained-glass rose window, and a fine beamed ceiling. The seminary grounds are also the site of the **Grotto to the Virgin Mary,** located in a ravine known as Finn's Glen. Built in about 1910, the grotto was restored in 1993.

75 George L. Burg House N L

2279 Summit Ave.

Associated Architects and Engineers, 1964

This 1960s version of French Provincial was the last house built on Summit before infills began appearing in the 1970s.

POI F World War I Memorial N L

Western end of Summit Ave.

Holyoke Jemne and Davis, 1922

A granite shaft erected by the Daughters of the American Revolution in honor of the St. Paul and Ramsey County servicemen who died in World War I.

2 Ramsey Hill

Ramsey Hill

Located north of Summit Avenue and east of Dale Street, Ramsey Hill offers St. Paul's—and the Twin Cities'—greatest concentration of architect-designed, late nineteenth-century houses, many lying within one of the neighborhood's three historic districts. This gathering of Victorians is remarkable for its general level of preservation, its high architectural quality, and its extent. In few other places in the United States can you see, in one compact neighborhood, so many homes of this kind. On those extravagant summer days when the big houses drowse in their deep green yards, it is hard—at least for any midwesterner—to think of a more pleasant residential environment.

The early settlers here, among them Ohio-born Jeremiah Selby, established farms beginning in the 1840s. By 1854, however, eager developers had already platted the neighborhood for residential use. As it turned out, only a few homes were built in the 1850s, mainly along or near Summit and Dayton avenues. Financial panics in 1857 and 1873 also slowed development, as did the lack of good public transportation connecting Ramsey Hill to the downtown area. The housing boom finally arrived in the 1880s, along with cable cars and later streetcars on Selby Avenue, the neighborhood's main commercial thoroughfare. Close to downtown but protected by bluffs from commercial or industrial sprawl, Ramsey Hill quickly became prime territory for upper middle-class settlement, especially along the streets south of Selby. Large homes and apartments were also built to the immediate north of Selby, along Dayton and Marshall avenues.

More so than Summit Hill to the south, Ramsey Hill features a broad range of building types, including row houses, apartments, residential hotels, churches, schools, and institutional structures. Among the noteworthy buildings here are Christ's Household of Faith (originally St. Joseph's Academy), parts of which date to 1863; the castlelike Lasher-Newell House (1864); Laurel Terrace (1887); Blair House (1887), a large apartment hotel; and the Cass Gilbert–designed Dayton Avenue Presbyterian Church (1888).

POI A Interstate 94 Corridor and Rondo Avenue Neighborhood

I-94 between Rice St. and Lexington Pkwy.

This stretch of Interstate 94, which opened in 1967, was created by carving a block-wide gash between Rondo (now Concordia) and St. Anthony Aves., often described as the heart of St. Paul's historic black community. Yet it's worth noting that the old Rondo neighborhood was, in fact, quite mixed, with many whites—often from immigrant groups—among its residents. It was also architecturally diverse and included fine homes as well as others that could fairly be described as slums. By the time the interstate came through, however, blacks did indeed bear the brunt of the impact, accounting for 75 percent of the people displaced by its construction.

1 St. Paul College

235 Marshall Ave.

Ellerbe Architects, 1964

Originally known as the St. Paul Vocational-Technical Institute, this drab period piece is situated across Dayton Ave. from the St. Paul Cathedral and does nothing to complement that monument. On the other hand, its blandness may be a defensible strategy, since the architects probably felt it was better to tread unobtrusively in the great church's shadow than to attempt a bold statement. The building has slit-like windows and a vaguely oppressive air, although a glassy cafeteria facing Summit Ave.

opens up the design a bit. Inside, the building is noted for its flexible use of space.

Christ's Household of Faith

2 Christ's Household of Faith (St. Joseph's Academy) N L

355 Marshall Ave.

1863 / additions, 1871, 1877, and 1884 (Edward P. Bassford) / chapel and library wing, John W. Wheeler, ca. 1930

These stone and brick buildings were for more than 100 years home to St. Joseph's Academy, a day and, at one time, boarding school for girls. Parts of the complex date to 1863, making it the state's oldest Catholic school building. It is also the largest surviving example of Italianate-style architecture in the Twin Cities.

The academy was founded in 1851 by the Sisters of St. Joseph of Carondelet, who 12 years later opened their first building here: a three-story stone structure with mild Italianate detailing (including a circular window beneath the front gable) at the southwest corner of the site. Additions followed to the north and east, also in the Italianate style. The most impressive section, constructed in 1877, is immediately to the east of the original building along Marshall. Four stories high, it features paired windows and a central two-story bay. Although the detailing is once again Italianate, this building—if its window proportions were altered a bit and the bay removed—might pass for an example of the Renaissance Revival style to come. The additions to the north date to the 1930s, by which time the academy functioned solely as a high school. The academy closed in 1972 because of declining enrollment. The complex was later

acquired by Christ's Household of Faith, a religious community that uses the buildings for a school and as living quarters.

POI B Historic Hill District N L

Created in 1976, this is St. Paul's oldest and largest locally designated historic district, taking in all or part of about 70 blocks. The district is roughly bounded by Interstates 35E and 94 and Dale St., although a section also extends west along Summit and Portland Aves. Much of this area falls within the boundaries of a nationally designated historic district of the same name that includes a sizable portion of the Summit Hill neighborhood as well. A much smaller national district, Woodland Park, also overlaps the local district along Dayton and Marshall Aves.

3 Aberdeen Condominiums L

370 Marshall Ave.

Collaborative Design Group, 2005

A nostalgic condominium building modeled on center-court apartments from the early twentieth century. It would have looked better with a well-defined cornice.

Aberdeen Hotel, 1937

LOST 1 *The condominiums are named after the **Aberdeen Hotel**, an eight-story residential hotel that once stood a block away at the southwest corner of Dayton Ave. and Virginia St. Designed by Willcox and Johnston, the Aberdeen opened in 1889 and initially attracted a well-heeled residential clientele. But the hotel's fortunes gradually declined, and it was a vacant hulk by the time of its demolition in 1944.*

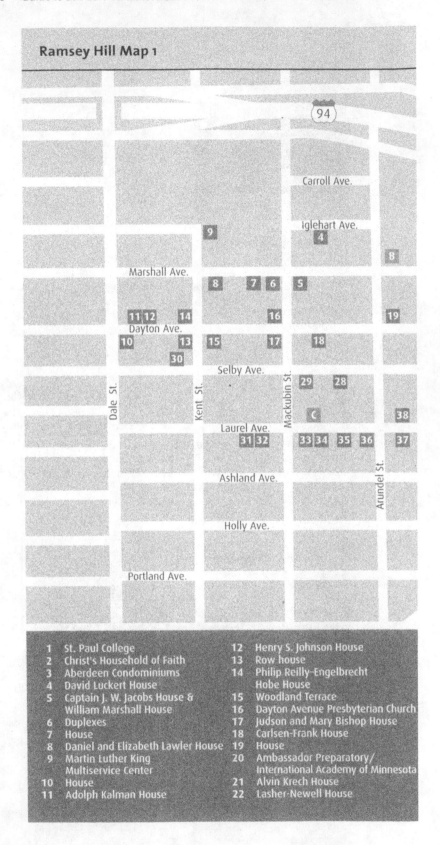

Ramsey Hill Map 1

1	St. Paul College	12	Henry S. Johnson House
2	Christ's Household of Faith	13	Row house
3	Aberdeen Condominiums	14	Philip Reilly-Engelbrecht
4	David Luckert House		Hobe House
5	Captain J. W. Jacobs House &	15	Woodland Terrace
	William Marshall House	16	Dayton Avenue Presbyterian Church
6	Duplexes	17	Judson and Mary Bishop House
7	House	18	Carlsen-Frank House
8	Daniel and Elizabeth Lawler House	19	House
9	Martin Luther King	20	Ambassador Preparatory/
	Multiservice Center		International Academy of Minnesota
10	House	21	Alvin Krech House
11	Adolph Kalman House	22	Lasher-Newell House

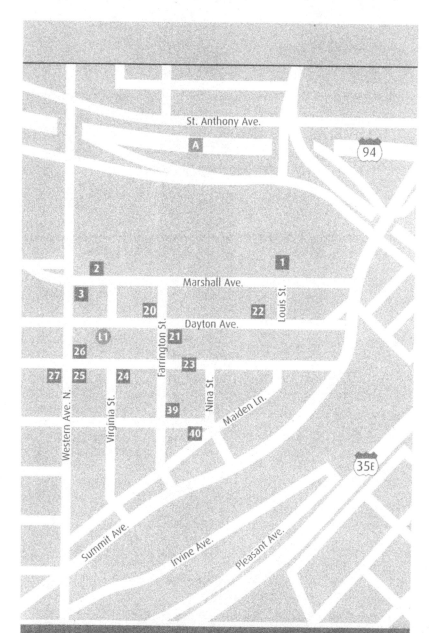

St. Anthony Ave.

A

94

Ramsey Hill

2

1

Marshall Ave.

Louis St.

3

20

22

Dayton Ave.

Farrington St.

L1

21

26

23

27   25   24

Nina St.

Western Ave. N.

Virginia St.

Maiden Ln.

39

40

35E

Summit Ave.

Irvine Ave.

Pleasant Ave.

23	Selby Avenue	36	Archibald Guthrie House
24	Virginia Street Church	37	Wilbur and Ada Howard House
25	W. A. Frost Building	38	Dr. William Davis House
26	YWCA Of St. Paul	39	Houses
27	Blair House	40	Laurel Terrace
28	St. Paul Curling Club		
29	Happy Gnome Restaurant		
30	Trott-Birch House	A	Interstate 94 Corridor and Rondo Avenue Neighborhood
31	Double houses		
32	Condominiums	B	Historic Hill District
33	Cornelius Kolff House	C	Fitzgerald Condominiums
34	Andrew Muir House		
35	William Howard House	L1	Aberdeen Hotel

Ramsey Hill Map 2

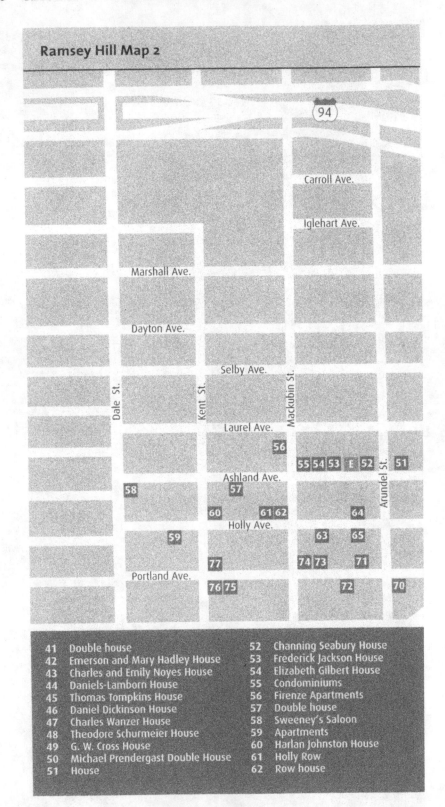

41 Double house
42 Emerson and Mary Hadley House
43 Charles and Emily Noyes House
44 Daniels-Lamborn House
45 Thomas Tompkins House
46 Daniel Dickinson House
47 Charles Wanzer House
48 Theodore Schurmeier House
49 G. W. Cross House
50 Michael Prendergast Double House
51 House

52 Channing Seabury House
53 Frederick Jackson House
54 Elizabeth Gilbert House
55 Condominiums
56 Firenze Apartments
57 Double house
58 Sweeney's Saloon
59 Apartments
60 Harlan Johnston House
61 Holly Row
62 Row house

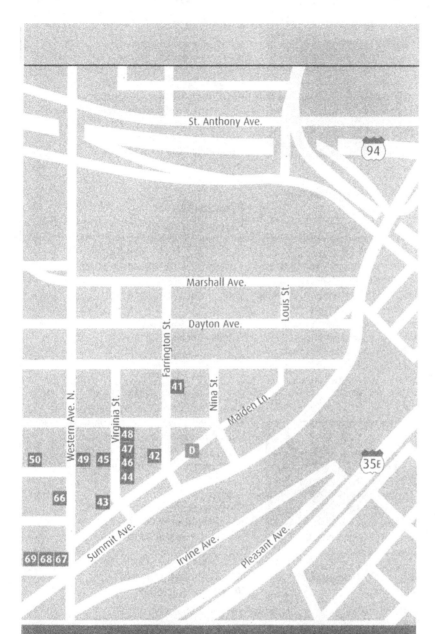

St. Anthony Ave.

94

Marshall Ave.

Louis St.

Dayton Ave.

Farrington St.

Ramsey Hill

41

Nina St.

Maiden Ln.

Western Ave. N.

Virginia St.

48
47
46
44

42

D

50   49   45

35E

66   43

Summit Ave.

69 68 67

Irvine Ave.

Pleasant Ave.

63	William George–Louisa McQuillan House	73	House
64	Everett Bailey House	74	Charles Bigelow III House & Fred R. Bigelow House
65	J. Walter Stevens House	75	Oscar Taylor Double House
66	Commodore Hotel	76	Portland Terrace
67	James and Annie Skinner House	77	St. John the Evangelist Episcopal Church
68	House		
69	Paul Doty House		
70	Arundel Apartments	D	Maiden Lane
71	Kirke-Murphy House	E	House
72	John White House		

David Luckert House

4 David (George) Luckert House N L

480 Iglehart Ave.

David Luckert, 1858

This mildly Federal-style home is one of the oldest buildings in the Historic Hill District, located along what used to be St. Anthony Rd., an early stagecoach route that linked St. Paul to Minneapolis. David Luckert, a German immigrant and skilled mason, constructed the house out of locally quarried limestone.

Captain J. W. Jacobs (left) & William Marshall Houses

5 Captain J. W. Jacobs House N L

492 Marshall Ave.

John H. Healy (builder), 1891

William Marshall House N L

496 Marshall Ave.

John H. Healy (builder), 1891

A pair of pattern book Queen Annes, neither of which suffers from a shortage of surface detail. The house at 496 was built for William R. Marshall, who after returning from the Civil War served as governor of Minnesota between 1866 and 1870.

6 Duplexes N L

512–14 Marshall Ave. and 233–35, 237–39 North Mackubin St.

J. Walter Stevens?, 1908

These three duplexes, which are similar but have different parapet and porch designs, offer a well-detailed version of the Mission Revival style that enjoyed a brief fling in the Twin Cities around 1910.

7 House N L

530 Marshall Ave.

ca. 1875–80

A pretty Italianate house, restored after being encased for years in aluminum siding.

8 Daniel and Elizabeth Lawler House N L

546 Marshall Ave.

John Coxhead, 1889

An imposing brick Queen Anne, fairly sedate by Coxhead's standards, with a hefty tower to one side and a two-story porch to the other. An oblong, shingle-clad attic dormer that curves out from the roofline is among the house's most distinctive features. The original owner, Daniel Lawler, was a Yale-trained lawyer who served as mayor of St. Paul from 1908 to 1910.

9 Martin Luther King Multiservice Center

270 North Kent St.

Adkins and Jackels Associates, ca. 1971

Architects in the 1970s loved to create jagged volumes of concrete and glass in a rugged style sometimes called Brutalism. Like many buildings of its era, this one probably proved more appealing to the architectural profession than to the community it was designed to serve.

10 House N L

614 Dayton Ave.

John Coxhead, 1888

Coxhead could always be counted on to do things a bit oddly, and here he offers up an angled, weirdly shaped tower that seems to be jammed into one corner of the house. Note the scrolling ornament beneath the tower's steep, pinched roof. The upper and lower front porches are modern reconstructions.

11 Adolph Kalman House N *L*

611 Dayton Ave.

William Thomas, 1890

A tall brick and stone Romanesque Revival house with an impressive front gable, a double-arched porch, and a tower that, for some reason, lurks well back along one side.

12 Henry S. Johnson House N *L*

601 Dayton Ave.

Clarence H. Johnston, 1889

An intriguing house with several distinctive touches, most notably the flared twin gables that curl down to the eaves like tiny ski jumps. Note also how the symmetry of the second story plays off the slight asymmetry of the first. The front porch roof originally had a decorative railing that added much to the overall design.

13 Row house N *L*

568–74 Dayton Ave.

Louis Lockwood, 1904

What a difference 16 years can make. Woodland Terrace just down the street is a model of Victorian exuberance. This row house, by contrast, is designed in the sedate and refined Georgian Revival style that became popular around 1900.

14 Philip Reilly–Engelbrecht Hobe House N *L*

565 Dayton Ave.

Abraham M. Radcliffe, 1881

A restored, richly ornamented wood-frame house built by lumber dealer Philip Reilly, who undoubtedly got a good deal on all of the brackets, scallops, modillions, balustrades, and whatnot

that make this one of St. Paul's most elaborate houses of its type. The house's overall form is Italianate, but much of the detailing—such as the incised carving and

Philip Reilly–Engelbrecht Hobe House

intricate bargeboards—is Eastlake. One of the house's later owners was Engelbrecht Hobe, a leader of St. Paul's Norwegian community who served for many years as consul to Sweden and Norway.

Woodland Terrace

15 Woodland Terrace N *L*

550–56 Dayton Ave. (also 198 North Kent St.)

B. J. Buechner?, 1889 / renovated, ca. 1980s

A row house with patterned red brickwork, sandstone staircases and trim, cast-iron ornament atop the gables, leaded-glass transoms, and just about everything else you'd expect of a Victorian dressed to kill. The deep-set arched entryways to the five townhomes are Romanesque Revival in character, but the building's busy roofline is of the Queen Anne persuasion.

16 Dayton Avenue Presbyterian Church N *L*

505 Dayton Ave. (also 217 North Mackubin St.)

Gilbert and Taylor, 1888 / addition, Thomas Holyoke, 1911

Cass Gilbert's mother, Elizabeth, was a founder of this congregation

Ramsey Hill

and no doubt helped her son's firm secure the commission for this church. Clad in Lake Superior sandstone from Wisconsin, the church is a strong design in the manner of H. H. Richardson,

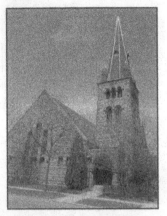

Dayton Avenue Presbyterian Church

whose work influenced Gilbert and almost every other architect in the United States. The rather squat corner tower is nicely integrated into the east side of the church, but the arched entry porch facing Dayton looks as though it was tacked on at the last minute. Within, there's a column-free auditorium with radial seating beneath a vaulted ceiling. An educational wing was added to the north of the church in 1911.

Judson and Mary Bishop House

17 Judson and Mary Bishop House N L

193 North Mackubin St. (at Dayton Ave.)

Abraham M. Radcliffe, 1882

No, Norman Bates doesn't live here, but if the psycho from *Psycho* was in the market for real estate in the Twin Cities, this French Second Empire pile might be the house of his dreams. It's a

late example of the style, carried out with no shortage of exuberance. Although the house is essentially rectangular, an assortment of bays and angled projections forestalls any foursquare monotony, while no fewer than 11 pedimented dormers jut out from the mansard roof. There was once a well-decorated front porch, but it was replaced years ago. The house was built by Judson Wade Bishop, an engineer and Civil War general who later became manager of the St. Paul and Sioux City Railroad, among other business endeavors. He also built and owned the Bishop Block, located in the Lowertown area of downtown St. Paul and now gone except for its front facade, which is incorporated into Galtier Plaza.

Carlsen-Frank House

18 Carlsen-Frank House N L

482 Dayton Ave.

Peter Carlsen and Sylvia Frank, 1979

A witty infill house, teetering on the brink of pop architecture and therefore much more interesting than the soberly nostalgic stuff now being built in the Hill District. Designed and owned by architects Peter Carlsen and Sylvia Frank, the house features a sweeping roofline and a windowless corner cylinder that calls to mind the towers of nearby Victorians. Cinched around the house is a broad white belt course that swoops up and over a round window on the east side before ending in an arrow, the meaning of which is left for the viewer to interpret. Overall, the house shows the influence of Philadelphia architect Robert Venturi, a leading postmodern guru.

19 House

409 Dayton Ave.

1878

A dainty Italianate house that's both older and more modest than most of its neighbors. It was moved to this site in the 1960s and has been nicely restored.

20 Ambassador Preparatory / International Academy of Minnesota (Frank and Anna Shepard House) *L*

325 Dayton Ave.

1882 / additions, ca. 1960s, 2006

A clunky 1960s addition hasn't helped the appearance of this substantial Queen Anne house, originally owned by Frank Shepard and his wife, Anna. Shepard was the son of David Shepard, who built much of the Great Northern Railway for James J. Hill. David Shepard resided in a large house (gone) across the street at 324 Dayton. Another big home built for a member of the family—Frank's son, David—is next door at 341 Dayton. It dates to 1901 and was designed by Louis Lockwood.

Alvin Krech House

21 Alvin Krech House N *L*

314 Dayton Ave.

Mould and McNicol, 1888 / restored, SALA Architects (Steve Buetow) and Robert Roscoe, 1996 and later

Another house with ties to the Shepard family, built at a cost of $24,000 for David Shepard's son-in-law, Alvin Krech. The architects, Charles Mould and Robert McNicol, designed several other St. Paul mansions (most notably the magnificent John Merriam House that once stood near the State Capitol), but here they produced a real oddity. The house's rugged stone exterior and arched first-floor windows are typical of the Romanesque Revival style, but the cubic shape and almost flat roof are not. Most peculiar of all is the third floor, which features inset porches supported by dwarf columns with overscaled Byzantine capitals. The house was subdivided in the 1930s into a nest of ten apartments. It stayed that way until 1996, when a couple bought it for ten dollars under a city revitalization program and then restored it as a single-family home.

Lasher-Newell House

22 Lasher-Newell House N *L*

251 Dayton Ave.

1864 / additions, J. Walter Stevens, 1886

A man's home is his castle, and this mighty stone house, with its tower and battlements, looks well equipped to repel invading hordes. Its central section, distinguished by prominent window hoods, dates to 1864 and is in the French Second Empire style. The house's tower, porte cochere, and western wing weren't built until 1886, after Stanford Newell acquired the house from its first owner, a man named Lasher about whom little is known except that he was a "money lender." Architect J. Walter Stevens did a superb job of blending the new with the old while also distinguishing them in subtle ways. For example, while the additions are built of the same limestone as the original house, the newer stone has a different finish. A lawyer and civic activist with political connections, Newell served as U.S. minister to the Netherlands from 1897 to 1906.

He was also a member of the St. Paul Park Board. In 1908 Newell Park in the Hamline-Midway neighborhood was named in his honor.

23 Selby Avenue

Nina St. to Dale St.

Platted in 1854, this historic avenue—long associated with the city's black community—is named after Jeremiah Selby, who owned an early farm on what is now the site of the St. Paul Cathedral. The avenue's character was largely determined by mass transit. St. Paul's first cable car line opened on Selby in 1887 and ran as far west as St. Albans St. It was electrified ten years later. Commercial and apartment development followed the streetcars, especially along the eastern end of the avenue.

Although not quite as bustling as Grand Ave. to the south, Selby retained a comfortable mix of homes, apartments, and businesses into the 1950s. By the 1960s, however, the avenue began to decline, in part because of dislocation caused by construction of Interstate 94 a few blocks to the north. A lack of new investment, a rising crime rate, and a racial disturbance in 1968 also contributed to the avenue's problems. In recent years, however, Selby has come back to life with new businesses and new housing. Architecturally, the eastern end of Selby (between Summit Ave. and Dale St.) remains the most interesting.

24 Virginia Street (Swedenborgian) Church N L

170 Virginia St. (also 338 Selby Ave.)

Gilbert and Taylor, 1887 / addition, Clarence H. Johnston, 1922

One of Cass Gilbert's most charming works, as dainty as a child's playhouse and alive with small, sweet details. It has a base of river boulders, clapboard walls, shingled gables, and an octagonal bell tower featuring delicate lancet windows and a spire sporting what may well be St. Paul's tiniest dormers. Note the equally miniscule eyebrow windows on the main roof. Inside,

Virginia Street Church

there's a barrel-vaulted sanctuary with stenciled decoration. The parish hall added to the east end of the church in 1922 is faithful to the original design. The Swedenborgian congregation that built and still occupies this church was organized in 1873 and was originally known as the St. Paul Society of the New Jerusalem Church.

W. A. Frost Building

25 W. A. Frost (Dacotah) Building N L

366–74 Selby Ave.

Hennessey, Agnew and Cox (builders), 1889 / renovated, J. E. Erickson and Sons, 1975

A pleasing Victorian commercial-apartment building with walls of dark red brick rising above a base of pink Ohio sandstone. Oriel windows dance along upper floors in a seemingly random pattern, adding to the building's charms. Originally known as the Dacotah Building, it takes its current name from a drugstore once located on the ground floor. The building was among the first in the Hill District to be renovated as the neighborhood began its turnaround in the 1970s.

26 YWCA of St. Paul *L*

375 Selby Ave. (also 198 Western Ave. North)

ca. 1880 and later / renovated and enlarged, Ankeny Kell Richter, 1992

A group of small buildings constructed between 1880 and 1920 are incorporated into this popular YWCA. The oldest buildings—a pair of Victorians from the early 1880s, including a three-story commercial block designed by pioneer St. Paul architect Abraham M. Radcliffe—are around the corner on Dayton Ave. Next door at 370 Dayton is a nifty little building designed in 1919 by Herbert Sullwold that features mosaic and tile decoration.

27 Blair House (Albion Hotel, Angus Hotel) N *L*

165 Western Ave. North (at Selby Ave.)

Hermann Kretz and William Thomas, 1887 and later / renovated, W. W. Orfield and Associates, ca. 1980s

Selby Ave.'s largest Victorian—not the subtlest design you'll ever see but great fun nevertheless. With its rugged stone base, patterned brickwork, zooming turrets, ornate parapets and gables, pressed metal bays, and round corner tower (minus its original cap), the building is a catalog of Victorian styles. Yet for all its architectural embroidery, the building's layout is quite rational, its large mass carved into four manageable sections by deep, narrow light courts. The architect, Hermann Kretz, made a specialty of apartment buildings, designing them all across St. Paul in the 1880s and 1890s.

The building is named after the man who commissioned it, Frank Blair, secretary of the St. Paul Improvement Co., a real estate firm. Blair lost his naming rights just six years later, in 1893, when the building became the Albion Hotel. In 1911 it was purchased by Twin Cities transit tycoon Thomas Lowry, who renamed it the Angus Hotel. After years of decline as a residential hotel, the building closed in 1971 and faced possible demolition. In the 1980s, however, as the Hill District began to flourish, the building was renovated. It's now home to condominium units as well as commercial tenants.

28 St. Paul Curling Club *L*

470 Selby Ave.

Clarence H. Johnston, 1913 / remodeled, 1982 and later

Home to the largest member-owned curling club in the United

Blair House

States. An organization known as the Nushka Club first curled (if that's the right word) on this site in the 1880s. In 1912 the club merged with another group to form the St. Paul Curling Club, which then constructed this building.

29 Happy Gnome Restaurant (Engine House No. 5) *L*

498 Selby Ave.

Abraham M. Radcliffe, 1882 / addition, J. A. Clark, 1886

One of St. Paul's oldest surviving fire stations, complete with corner bell tower. It was built as Engine House No. 5 and expanded four years later to accommodate a ladder company as well. Last used as a fire station in 1930, the building went through a number of uses until it was converted to a restaurant in 1979.

Il Vesco Vino Restaurant

30 Trott-Birch House N *L*

579 Selby Ave.

Hermann Kretz and Co., 1890

This Chateauesque double house is a rarity in the Twin Cities because of its height—a full three stories, with a fourth tucked beneath the steep roof. Three-story houses are more commonly found in denser eastern cities like Boston. The rigorously symmetrical main facade culminates in a pair of gabled dormers to which floral ornaments are pinned like giant boutonnieres. A real estate dealer was the first owner of the

house, suggesting that it was built as a rental property.

534 Laurel Ave.

31 Double houses N *L*

524–26, 534 Laurel Ave.

John Coxhead, 1888

A pair of idiosyncratic double houses that look to have been identical originally. Atop each of the houses' distinctive oval towers is one of Coxhead's signature elements—an absurdly high, steep roof that resembles the mouthpiece of a cigarette holder blown up to enormous scale. You'll find a similar tower and roof on a Coxhead-designed house at 614 Dayton Ave.

32 Condominiums (Summit Lodge No. 163) N *L*

512 Laurel Ave.

Edward P. Bassford, 1891

This building originally served as a Masonic lodge. It is one of two historic Masonic lodges—the other is the Triune Temple in the Merriam Park neighborhood—that survive in St. Paul.

POI C Fitzgerald Condominiums (San Mateo Flats) ! N *L*

475–81 Laurel Ave.

Frederick A. Clarke, 1894 / addition (porches), Louis Lockwood, ca. 1905

A pair of standard late Victorian apartment buildings that carry one of the most famous addresses in St. Paul for the simple reason that F. Scott Fitzgerald was born in an apartment on the second floor of 481 Laurel on September 24, 1896. At the time of Fitzger-

Fitzgerald Condominiums

ald's birth, the apartments were almost new, and while they were certainly decent enough, they were hardly among the neighborhood's tonier residences. He lived here with his parents until 1898, when the family moved to Buffalo, NY, where they stayed for ten years before returning to St. Paul.

Now known as the Fitzgerald Condominiums, the buildings (originally sixplexes) were eventually subdivided into 24 apartments and by 1970 were plagued by crime and drug problems. A few years later, however, 12 urban pioneers bought the buildings and renovated them, restoring the apartments to their original size. Among the first projects of its kind in the Hill District, it provided a model for many renovations to come. In 2004, 481 Laurel earned another distinction by becoming the first building in the Twin Cities to be designated a national Literary Landmark by the Friends of Libraries U.S.A.

33 Cornelius Kolff House N *L*

472 Laurel Ave.

Charles W. Mould, 1884

An unusually plain house compared to most of the Victorians along Laurel. It's likely that the front porch and the shingled portion above it are additions from the later 1880s.

34 Andrew Muir House N *L*

466 Laurel Ave.

Augustus Gauger, 1893

An impressively detailed house that shows how the Queen Anne style of the 1880s (evident here in the corner tower and complex roofline) morphed into the Colonial Revival of the 1890s. One of the house's more curious features is a horizontal band over the front porch with an asymmetric arrangement of two windows and three carved panels. Andrew Muir was a contractor who seven years earlier had built an even larger house at 545 Summit Ave. That house, also designed by Gauger, was demolished in 1944.

William Howard House

35 William Howard House N *L*

452 Laurel Ave.

ca. 1880

This Victorian dollhouse was probably built from a pattern book, and its modest size is part of what makes it so charming.

36 Archibald Guthrie House N *L*

444 Laurel Ave.

ca. 1880 / rebuilt, Kenneth Worthen, 1924

A complete makeover, and a very nice one at that, of an 1880s house. Architect Kenneth Worthen was a master of the Period Revival styles popular in the 1920s, and this house displays his talent for assembling pictur-esque elements into a captivat-ing design.

37 Wilbur and Ada Howard House N *L*

422 Laurel Ave.

1882 / enlarged, Denslow W. Millard, 1887

A visual encyclopedia of Victorian gingerbread. Sawn, turned, and carved woodwork sashays along the porch, around the windows, beneath the eaves, and even above the basement walls. Top-ping it all is a weird, towerlike roof projection with a large dormer.

38 Dr. William Davis House N *L*

411 Laurel Ave.

Cass Gilbert, 1883

Another of Gilbert's early St. Paul houses. Its modest, Shingle Style demeanor must have been strik-ing at a time when most new houses in the neighborhood were anything but understated. It was built for a physician whose brother-in-law, Thomas Holyoke, was a draftsman in Gilbert's office.

39 Houses N *L*

301, 307, 313 Laurel Ave.

1882–84 / restored, Robert Engstrom, ca. 1980

The Hill District's only identical triplets, known in the neigh-borhood as the "three sisters." Aside from their paint jobs, the one noticeable difference among them is that the house at 313 Laurel lacks a side porch,

301 Laurel Ave.

though it presumably had one originally.

40 Laurel Terrace (Riley Row) ! N *L*

286–94 Laurel Ave.

Willcox and Johnston, 1887

One of the finest Victorian row houses in the United States, beautifully situated at the slightly skewed corner of Laurel Ave. and Nina St. Built for $75,000, Laurel Terrace was a luxurious building for its day. With its bold lines, strong colors, and wealth of orna-ment, it is almost startling in its intensity. The Richardsonian Romanesque style was seldom used for large row houses: Laurel Terrace is so unusual in this re-gard that it's been illustrated in at least two major guidebooks to American architecture. William Willcox and Clarence Johnston had been together for less than a year when they designed the row house, and it remains the great-est surviving monument of their brief (1886–89) but productive partnership.

Although it has no shortage of ornament, Laurel Terrace derives its power and presence from the simplicity of its basic forms. Unlike most Victorians, it has a strong horizontal emphasis, with each of its three stories de-fined by a different design ele-ment. On the ground floor, deep entrance arches dominate the composition. The second story features carefully grouped win-dows of similar size and shape. The third floor offers a line of crisp gables to demarcate each of the original seven apartments. Tying the design together like a

Laurel Terrace

giant hinge is an inset corner tower topped by a steep conical roof outfitted with Gothic dormers. The impeccable detailing—in sandstone, granite, brick, slate, copper, wrought iron, and stained glass—includes a variety of carved creatures. The building also came equipped with its own powerhouse (located along Maiden Ln. to the rear and now an apartment).

Originally named after its first owner, William C. Riley, who was in the telegraph business and who lived across the street, at 291 Laurel, Laurel Terrace can claim F. Scott Fitzgerald as its most famous former resident. As a boy, Fitzgerald lived in the row house between 1908 and 1909, first with his maternal grandmother and later with his parents.

156–58 North Farrington St.

41 Double house N *L*

156–58 North Farrington St.

Albert Zschocke, 1888

A wonderful design from the short-lived Albert Zschocke. This large double house is full of fanciful touches, including a front gable that swoops down into a pair of improbable curlicues, a

long eyebrow window peering out from the roof, and a rounded corner tower with inset brick cylinders that are peculiar even by Victorian standards. As with most of Zschocke's work, the overall effect is very romantic.

42 Emerson and Mary Hadley House N *L*

123 North Farrington St.

Cass Gilbert, 1895

Another example of Gilbert's ability to dress up a two-story box in the style of the moment—in this case Georgian Revival—and do it better than just about anyone else in St. Paul. The pedimented window above the portico is particularly fine. Emerson Hadley was a lawyer whose partner, James Armstrong, also commissioned a house from Gilbert (at 506 Grand Hill).

Maiden Lane

POI D Maiden Lane

West of Summit Ave. between Selby and Western Aves.

This picturesque little byway is essentially an alley for Summit Ave., and it's one of the few places in the Twin Cities where you feel as though you might have stumbled upon a tiny piece of Europe somehow transported across the pond. At one time, there were over 15 large carriage houses here. The lane's rough brick pavement, numerous walls and gates, and large Victorian carriage houses combine to create a unique environment. It was probably named after a famous street in the Covent Garden section of London that at various times was home to such luminaries as Benjamin Disraeli, Voltaire, the poet Andrew Marvell, and the painter J. M. W. Turner.

Charles and Emily Noyes House

43 Charles and Emily Noyes House N *L*

89 Virginia St.

Gilbert and Taylor, 1887

Very probably St. Paul's first high-style Colonial Revival house. Cass Gilbert once worked for the New York firm of McKim, Mead and White, which introduced Colonial Revival on the East Coast, and so it's hardly surprising that he imported the style to St. Paul. With its somewhat fussy detailing and elongated proportions, the house is by no means free of Victorian overtones. Even so, it must have been a novelty in its day. Charles Noyes founded a wholesale drug company known as Noyes Brothers and Cutler in Lowertown. He also had interests in banking and publishing. As a native of Connecticut and a member of the Sons of the American Revolution, Noyes would have been familiar with the historic houses of New England, and he probably didn't require any convincing from Gilbert to build a Colonial-inspired home of his own.

44 Daniels-Lamborn House N *L*

110 Virginia St.

1857 / remodeled and enlarged, Millard and Joy, 1891

The rear portion of this Colonial Revival house dates to 1857 and may well be the oldest property in the Historic Hill District. It was built at 267 Dayton Ave. for Joseph Daniels, an attorney. A later owner, Charles Lamborn, greatly enlarged the house in 1891, in part to accommodate a huge reception for his daughter's wedding. The house was moved here in 1907 to make way for the construction of Louis St., located just north of the St. Paul Cathedral.

45 Thomas Tompkins House N *L*

113 Virginia St.

J. Walter Stevens, 1890

A Colonial Revival house with hints of the Medieval in the front dormer, which is adorned with heavy bargeboards. Note also the exquisite carved shell above the attic windows.

46 Daniel Dickinson House N *L*

118 Virginia St.

ca. 1883

Stick Style houses aren't all that common in the Twin Cities, and this is one of the better examples, complete with carved sunflower motifs in the two front gables. The house's first owner was an associate justice of the Minnesota Supreme Court.

47 Charles Wanzer House N *L*

122 Virginia St.

ca. 1882

A picture-postcard Victorian with all the gingerbread your heart could desire. The house is clad in what is known as German siding, which differs from the usual clapboard in that the upper edge of each piece is concave and fits into a groove at the bottom of the piece above.

Theodore Schurmeier House

48 Theodore Schurmeier House N *L*

130 Virginia St.

Cass Gilbert, ca. 1884 / rebuilt, Cass Gilbert, ca. 1888

One of Gilbert's earliest St. Paul houses. It shows his embrace of the Shingle Style well in advance of most other local architects. The house was originally located at 189 Virginia but was moved here in about 1887 to make way for the now vanished Aberdeen Hotel. Gilbert altered the house somewhat after the move. It was built for Theodore Schurmeier, a dry goods wholesaler and banker who was married to a daughter of shoe manufacturer Conrad Gotzian, another of Gilbert's clients.

49 G. W. Cross (Henry and Margaret Castle) House N *L*

112 Western Ave. North

George Wirth, ca. 1885

This extensively reworked pile combines the usual roofline the-atrics with a largely symmetrical facade—not what you'd normally expect to find on a Queen Anne house. Among the home's early owners was Henry Castle, a jour-nalist who in 1912 published a three-volume history of St. Paul still valued by students of the city's past.

Michael Prendergast Double House

50 Michael Prendergast Double House N *L*

399–401 Ashland Ave.

Willcox and Johnston, 1887

A striking brick and stone double house that applies a classical ap-pliqué to Romanesque Revival forms. The contrasting colors of the checkerboard frieze and arched entrances (which feature widely spaced quoins) make this one of the neighborhood's most vivid houses. Michael Prender-gast was in the plumbing supply business and built the house as a rental property.

431 Ashland Ave.

51 House N *L*

431 Ashland Ave.

Ole Ask (builder), 1890

This splendidly restored Queen Anne was moved here in 1977 from 825 Dayton Ave. Its builder, carpenter Ole Ask, may have taken the design from a pattern book, although the house is simi-lar to those produced by the local architectural team of Omeyer and Thori.

52 Channing Seabury House N *L*

453 Ashland Ave.

Mould and McNicol, 1887

A somewhat ungainly house most notable as the longtime

home of Channing Seabury, a public-minded wholesale grocer who led the commission that oversaw construction of the Minnesota State Capitol from 1893 to 1905. Seabury became a close friend of the capitol's architect, Cass Gilbert, who lived for a time just down the street.

POI E House N L

455–57 Ashland Ave.

1882 / addition, ca. 1979

U.S. Senator Paul Wellstone and his wife, Sheila, lived at 455 Ashland at the time of their death in a plane crash near Eveleth, MN, on October 25, 2002. The couple's daughter, Marcia, and five other people also perished in the accident.

Frederick Jackson House

53 Frederick Jackson House N L

467 Ashland Ave.

James Knox Taylor, 1882

A Shingle Style beauty by James Knox Taylor, who later partnered with Cass Gilbert. Taylor moved to Philadelphia in 1892 and later became supervising architect of the U.S. Treasury.

54 Elizabeth Gilbert House N L

471 Ashland Ave.

Cass Gilbert, 1884 / later remodelings

Cass Gilbert's first St. Paul house, built for his mother (although Gilbert himself lived here until his marriage in 1887). Gilbert began designing the house in 1882 when he was just 23 years old and working in Baltimore for the New York firm of McKim, Mead and White. In a letter to his friend and fellow architect Clarence

Johnston, he wrote: "I am trying to study the whole thing with a loving regard for those that are to occupy it. It has become a little

Elizabeth Gilbert House

problem to do something which shall be artistic, not fashionable, sensible, genuine, and a place I shall not tire of myself." On the whole, he met those goals, designing a house that, among other things, introduced the Shingle Style to St. Paul. Although the exterior has been modified (in a couple of instances by Gilbert himself), the interior remains largely intact.

55 Condominiums (St. John the Evangelist Episcopal Church) N L

495–99 Ashland Ave.

William H. Willcox (rear portion), 1883 / Thori, Alban and Fischer (front portion, St. Paul Universalist Church), 1907 / renovated, ca. 1980s

This stone structure was built as St. John the Evangelist Church and was later occupied by the St. Paul Universalist Church, Contender for the Faith Church, and other congregations. The rear portion, which has walls of gray rather than yellow limestone, is older than the church proper and was originally a school. Cass Gilbert and James Knox Taylor designed three additions to the first church here in the 1880s, but none of their work survives.

56 Firenze Apartments L

117 North Mackubin St.

James McLeod, 1900

A touch of Florence imported to St. Paul, and one of the Hill District's most distinctive build-

Firenze Apartments

ings. The highlight is a rooftop loggia that rises from corbelled brick arches and features red and green terra-cotta panels adorned with shields and other motifs. Note also the ornate chimneys at the four corners of the building and the cast-iron balcony above the front entrance. The architect of this exotic concoction, James McLeod, was also the son-in-law of its builder, Dr. Rudolph Schiffman, who lived nearby on Summit Ave. The apartments within are now condominiums.

57 Double house *L*

532–36 Ashland Ave.

Hermann Kretz and Co., 1890

Another very tall double house from Kretz, who seems to have had a patent on this sort of thing in St. Paul. The house's sandstone facade is also unusual for this neighborhood.

58 Sweeney's Saloon *L*

96 North Dale St.

Abraham M. Radcliffe, 1886 / renovated, ca. 1979

One of the Hill District's older commercial buildings, now a popular watering hole. Legend holds that it was once used as a brothel, though for many years it was the home of an establishment known as Sweeney's General Store.

59 Apartments *L*

578–80 Holly Ave.

ca. 1890

A pair of horseshoe arches dominates the front of this crisply detailed late Victorian building, which grafts Moorish and Renaissance Revival elements into a convincing composition. The

578–80 Holly Ave.

building once functioned as a dormitory for the Backus (later Oak Hall) School for Girls, a finishing school that operated next door until it closed in 1940.

60 Harlan Johnston House *N L*

72 North Kent St.

F. J. Jenny (builder), 1908

An unusual house for this part of St. Paul. The overall character is Arts and Crafts, though the house has more in common with English versions of the style than with the standard American bungalow that was beginning to flourish at this time.

Holly Row

61 Holly Row *N L*

505–9 Holly Ave.

James Chisholm, 1888 / renovated, 1970s

The very picture of a Victorian row house, clad in rock-faced sandstone. The tightly packed architectural crowd along the roofline includes four chimneys, two towers, a gable, and a dormer. Unsympathetic modern windows date to the 1970s, when the building was renovated following a fire.

62 Row house N *L*

501 Holly Ave. (also 71–79 North Mackubin St.)

ca. 1885–90 / renovated, 1978

In the early days of the historic preservation movement that began in the 1970s, inappropriate things were often done to old buildings to "restore" them. The no-nos in this case included sandblasting the brick walls, removing the original porches, and installing modern-style windows. Still, the work here shouldn't be judged too harshly, since the idea of historically "correct" restoration was just beginning to gain currency at the time.

63 William George–Louisa McQuillan House N *L*

472 Holly Ave.

1895

A rather daunting stone house that's one of several built in St. Paul for Louisa McQuillan, F. Scott Fitzgerald's wealthy and apparently restless maternal grandmother. Like her house of the same period at 623 Summit Ave., this one has crenellations (atop the front bay window) and conveys an aura of no-nonsense solidity. Playwright August Wilson once lived here.

64 Everett Bailey House N *L*

459 Holly Ave.

James Knox Taylor, 1885 / Art: Chimney Sweep (wood sculpture), Scott Showell

A house in an admirable mix of styles, completed by James Knox Taylor just before he became Cass Gilbert's partner. The original owner, Everett Bailey, was a banker who must have loved the place: he lived here until his death in 1953.

J. Walter Stevens House

65 J. Walter Stevens House N *L*

458 Holly Ave.

J. Walter Stevens, 1888

Designed by and for prominent St. Paul architect J. Walter Stevens, this house abounds in strange details such as the toothpick-thin porch columns, those on one side taller than those on the other. Note also the wide, thin eaves and the three tiny arched windows inserted into the center of the second story.

Commodore Hotel bar

66 Commodore Hotel N *L*

79 Western Ave. North

Alexander Rose, 1921 / bar, Werner Wittkamp, ca. 1940s

This gracious apartment hotel, now condominiums, is one of the largest buildings in the Hill District. Designed for a well-to-do clientele, the Commodore originally included a rooftop garden, a dining room, and other amenities. With its mild classical detailing and U-shaped, center-court layout, the building is typical of its time. One unusual feature (at least for St. Paul) is that the courtyard is walled and gated, creating a private area for residents. The building is attributed to Alexander Rose, a Scottish-born architect from Minneapolis who specialized in apartments. It was renovated and converted into condominiums following a 1978 gas explosion that caused heavy damage. Inside are the partial remains of a boffo art deco barroom designed by Werner Wittkamp. The Russian-born Wittkamp, trained as a set designer in Europe, produced a number of suave buildings and interiors in the Twin Cities in the 1930s and 1940s.

James and Annie Skinner House

67 James and Annie Skinner House N *L*

385 Portland Ave.

Clarence H. Johnston, 1902

This brick foursquare hints at a variety of styles—from Jacobethan to Colonial Revival to neoclassical—but doesn't really embrace any of them. Instead, it relies on powerful massing to achieve its considerable effect. Details of note include the monumental columns and piers of the front porch, chimneys with distinctive flared tops, and a carriage house connected to the main house via an open passageway. James Skinner, the original owner, was in the fur business and also involved in banking. During World War I, he was appointed by President Woodrow Wilson to a council that oversaw war purchases for the Allies, an assignment that sent him on a perilous voyage to London during the height of submarine warfare in the North Atlantic. The appointment came about because Skinner was a friend of one of Wilson's key advisers, Colonel Edward House, with whom he had roomed while both were students at Cornell University.

68 House N *L*

389 Portland Ave.

ca. 1906

A large if rather staid example of the Renaissance Revival style, delivered in light-colored brick with stone trim. The inset front porch is perhaps the design's most unusual feature.

Paul Doty House

69 Paul Doty House N *L*

427 Portland Ave.

Emmanuel Masqueray, 1915

One of only two houses in St. Paul known to have been designed by Emmanuel Masqueray, the French-born architect of the St. Paul Cathedral. With its exceptionally high roof and aura of continental suavity, the house certainly looks French, and it's not hard to imagine it standing somewhere on the outskirts of Paris. The highlight is a large front dormer that curves down into a parapet adorned with urns. Note also the French doors within the arcaded front porch. Finished at about the same time as the Cathedral opened, this may well have been Masqueray's last residential work before his death in 1917. The original owner, Paul Doty, was vice president and general manager of the St. Paul Gas and Light Co.

70 Arundel Apartments N *L*

436–38 Portland Ave.

1904

A monumental apartment building, unlike any other in the Twin

Charles Bigelow III (right) & Fred R. Bigelow Houses

Cities, with colossal Ionic porticos defining the two entries. The columns themselves—made of molded brick rather than the usual stone or wood—are also quite unusual.

71 Kirke-Murphy House N *L*

453 Portland Ave.

ca. 1889

A flamboyant brick-clad Queen Anne with patterned shingle work on the front gable and tower. Its first owner, William Kirke, lived here for only a few years before moving to a house at 629 Summit Ave.

72 John White House N *L*

460 Portland Ave.

Cass Gilbert, 1885

An early house by Gilbert that's hard to peg to any particular style, although Tudor and Renaissance Revival elements predominate. The front porch, with its interplay of thin columns and thick piers, is quite striking.

73 House N *L*

475 Portland Ave.

ca. 1890

A large Colonial Revival house with an elaborately landscaped side yard enclosed by an ornate iron fence. Among the one-time owners of this house was Maud Hill, who moved here after separating from her husband, Louis (son of James J.), in 1934.

74 Charles Bigelow III House N *L*

487 Portland Ave.

Thomas Holyoke, 1910

Fred R. Bigelow House N *L*

495 Portland Ave.

Thomas Holyoke, 1910

A pair of elegant Tudor Revivals designed for Charles Bigelow and son Fred by Cass Gilbert protégé Thomas Holyoke. The house at 495 Portland has exceptionally crisp stone trim and decorated bargeboards. Charles Bigelow was president of the St. Paul Fire and Marine Insurance Co. (now Travelers) from 1876 until 1911, when he was succeeded by his son, who ran the company until 1938.

75 Oscar Taylor Double House N *L*

544–46 Portland Ave.

Clarence H. Johnston, 1890

A dark, weighty double house, executed in rock-faced Lake Superior sandstone and very much in the spirit of H. H. Richardson. The tower, which has a recessed porch with a grillelike balustrade and dwarf columns beneath a witch's-hat roof, is one of the finest of its type in the Twin Cities.

76 Portland Terrace (Bookstaver Row House) N *L*

548–54 Portland Ave.

Gilbert and Taylor, 1888

Cass Gilbert's only surviving row house in St. Paul. The recessed arched entries on the building's eastern end and around the corner on Kent St. call to mind the work of H. H. Richardson, but overall the row house has the relaxed, comfortable feel of Colonial Revival. Among historic residents of the row house were

Portland Terrace

Edward and Mollie Fitzgerald, who conceived their famous son while living here in late 1895. Just south of this building, at 20–22 North Kent St., is a double house dating to 1889 that was also designed by Gilbert.

St. John the Evangelist Episcopal Church

77 St. John the Evangelist Episcopal Church N *L*

Portland Ave. at North Kent St.

Clarence H. Johnston, 1903 / remodeled, Clarence H. Johnston and Ralph Adams Cram, ca. 1919

guildhall, 60 North Kent St.

Cass Gilbert, 1895

This block-long church complex incorporates the work of both Cass Gilbert and Clarence Johnston. Gilbert's half-timbered guildhall along Kent St. was built first, in 1895, and served as a temporary worship space for the congregation, which moved that year from its old)church on Ashland Ave. By the time the congregation raised enough money to build a full-scale church in 1902, Gilbert had moved his practice to New York City, so Johnston received the commission. Built largely of local limestone, the church is dominated by a square tower with pinnacles at each corner—a type sometimes called a crown tower. Note the gargoyles, six to a side, that lurk near the top. Johnston was forced to extensively modify Gilbert's hall to fit it in with the new church. Inside, the church includes a beautiful chancel that's the product of a 1919 remodeling by Johnston and Boston architect Ralph Cram (designer of nearby House of Hope Presbyterian Church).

Ramsey Hill

3 Summit Hill

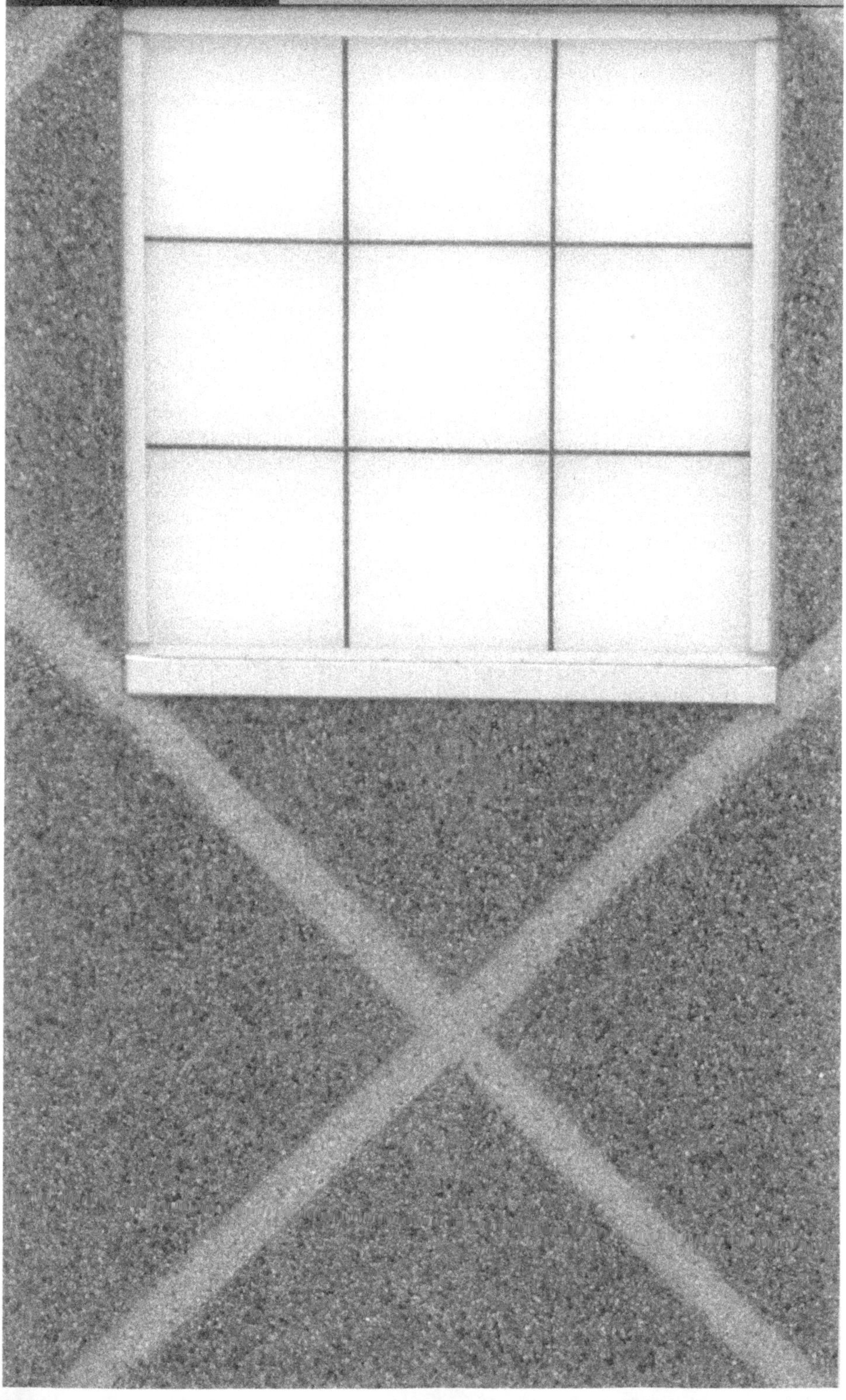

Summit Hill

This pleasant, well-kept neighborhood is almost exclusively residential, except for Grand Avenue, and it's one of St. Paul's showpieces. Popularly known as Crocus Hill, the neighborhood consists of block upon block of late nineteenth- and early twentieth-century houses, many of them quite large. Among the notable architects who designed homes here are Cass Gilbert, Clarence Johnston, Allen Stem, Louis Lockwood, and Augustus Gauger. Some of the finest houses are located along the curving, secluded streets—such as Crocus Place and Kenwood Parkway—that weave around the blufftops above Interstate 35E. Virtually all of the neighborhood is included in the federally designated Historic Hill District. The houses along Grand Hill, Heather Place, and Summit Court are also within the city preservation district of the same name.

As with most of the Twin Cities, Summit Hill developed in tandem with mass transportation. Horsecars began operating on Grand Avenue as early as 1872, spurring growth in the eastern part of the neighborhood. But it wasn't until the arrival of electric trolleys in 1890 that a true housing boom began here. Many of Summit Hill's larger homes were built between 1890 and 1910, when various Classical and Period Revival styles flourished. As a result, the neighborhood has a more sedate feel than Ramsey Hill to the north, where Queen Anne reigns. In the western portions of Summit Hill, past Victoria Street, the housing stock tends to be newer, much of it dating to between 1910 and 1930. Only a small number of modern houses have been inserted into the neighborhood's historic fabric, and overall Summit Hill has the feel of a place happily immune to the churning forces of urban change.

Among the neighborhood's outstanding works of architecture are the Frank B. Kellogg House (1890), a National Historic Landmark on Fairmount Avenue; the exotic Jared Howe House at 455 Grand Avenue (1907); the Goodkind Double House (1910) at 5–7 Heather Place; the Frank and Rosa Seifert House (1914), a Prairie School gem at 975 Osceola Avenue; and the Aberle House (1927) at 54 Crocus Place.

1 Grand Avenue

Dale St. to Lexington Pkwy.

Grand Ave. was platted in 1871 and began as a residential street, although it was never as ritzy as Summit Ave. a block to the north. The arrival of electric streetcars in 1890 touched off a long process of development by which Grand— now a vibrant blend of commercial and residential uses—took on its current form. Apartments and stores began to appear here by 1900, but much of Grand's best building stock dates to the 1920s, when auto dealers flocked to the avenue. Their garage and showroom buildings later proved ideal for conversion to upscale mini-malls. Many of the avenue's three-story brick apartment buildings are also from the 1920s.

Like other older commercial strips in St. Paul, Grand declined in the 1950s. But a renaissance fueled by the gentrification of the Historic Hill District in the 1970s turned everything around. Zoning changes also helped preserve the avenue's mix of housing and businesses. Today, Grand's most pressing problems appear to be parking and the proliferation of upscale chain stores, which critics see as a threat to the avenue's unique character. Architecturally, Grand is not especially remarkable, although its many small brick buildings tend to be of higher quality than those commonly found along other commercial streets in the Twin Cities.

2 Ivy League Condominiums N

625–35 Grand Ave.

Louis Lockwood, 1905

A trio of brick apartment buildings fronted by three-story porches, typical of Lockwood's designs from this period.

3 Ramaley Building N

656–66 Grand Ave.

ca. 1928

One of the more ornate Period Revival buildings on the avenue.

LOST 1 *Part of this site was once occupied by* **Ramaley Hall,** *built in about 1901. The upstairs was a popular spot for social events and also home to a dance school where F. Scott Fitzgerald took lessons when he was 13 years old.*

4 House (Peter Denzer Home and Studio)

814 Grand Ave.

1905 / addition, Peter Denzer, 1980

The simple front addition to this old house drew the wrath of the local architectural police, who deemed it quite awful. "Committed by supposedly artistic individuals, it is a serious crime," thundered the editor of a neighborhood newspaper. In truth, the addition's hand-built flavor adds some character to Grand, which has few architectural surprises. Nothing like Denzer's handiwork will ever appear again on the avenue: zoning rules were quickly changed to ban additions of this kind.

5 Victoria Crossing South (Byers-Patro Motor Co.)

850 Grand Ave.

John Alden, 1927 / renovated, ca. 1982

Victoria Crossing East (Bingham and Norton Co.)

851–57 Grand Ave.

Beaver Wade Day, 1915 / renovated, ca. 1980

Victoria Crossing West (Tilden Brothers Produce Co., Grand Avenue State Bank, Berry Chevrolet Co.)

861–67 Grand Ave. and 35 South Victoria St.

John Alden, 1922–23 / renovated, Jim Wengler, ca. 1974

Three of the four buildings at this intersection were once auto dealerships, selling such extinct species as Studebaker, Reo, and Erskine, as well as more familiar names like Plymouth and Chevrolet. The building at 850 Grand, home to the popular Cafe Latté, is the most sophisticated of the three, its decorative motifs suggesting the art deco style to come. Ornament of a different sort adorns the old Chevrolet dealership that's part of Victoria Crossing West. Here you'll find three white terra-cotta cartouches in a circle-and-tab design done in the intricate style of Louis Sullivan.

Victoria Crossing South

Summit Hill Map 1

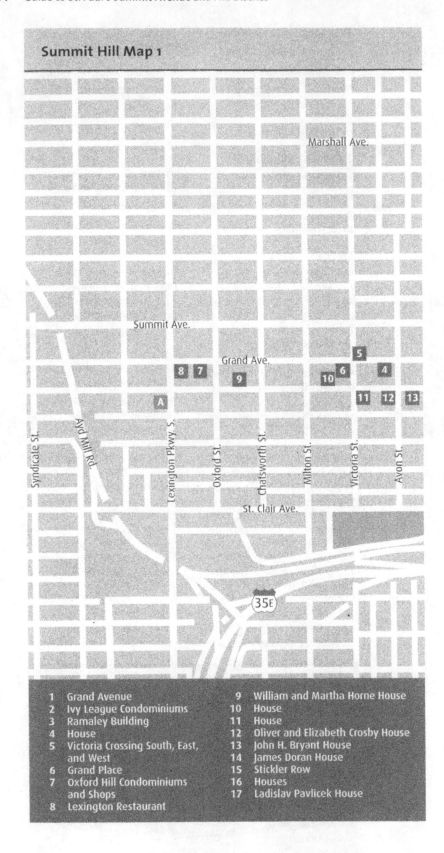

1	Grand Avenue	9	William and Martha Horne House
2	Ivy League Condominiums	10	House
3	Ramaley Building	11	House
4	House	12	Oliver and Elizabeth Crosby House
5	Victoria Crossing South, East, and West	13	John H. Bryant House
		14	James Doran House
6	Grand Place	15	Stickler Row
7	Oxford Hill Condominiums and Shops	16	Houses
		17	Ladislav Pavlicek House
8	Lexington Restaurant		

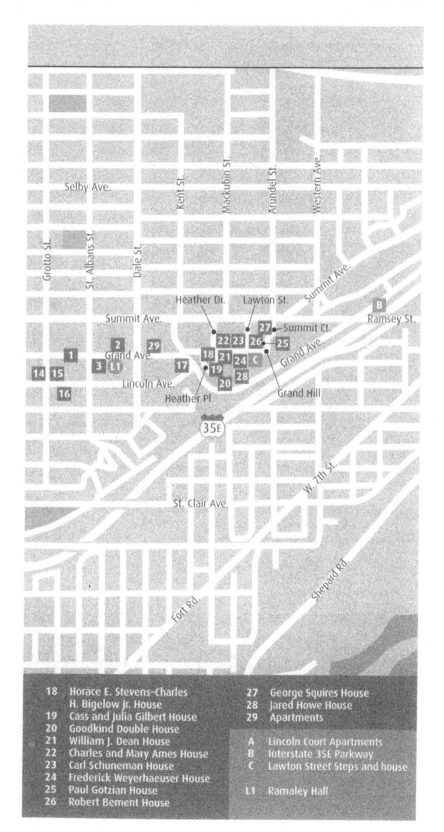

18 Horace E. Stevens–Charles
    H. Bigelow Jr. House
19 Cass and Julia Gilbert House
20 Goodkind Double House
21 William J. Dean House
22 Charles and Mary Ames House
23 Carl Schuneman House
24 Frederick Weyerhaeuser House
25 Paul Gotzian House
26 Robert Bement House

27 George Squires House
28 Jared Howe House
29 Apartments

A   Lincoln Court Apartments
B   Interstate 35E Parkway
C   Lawton Street Steps and house

L1 Ramaley Hall

Summit Hill

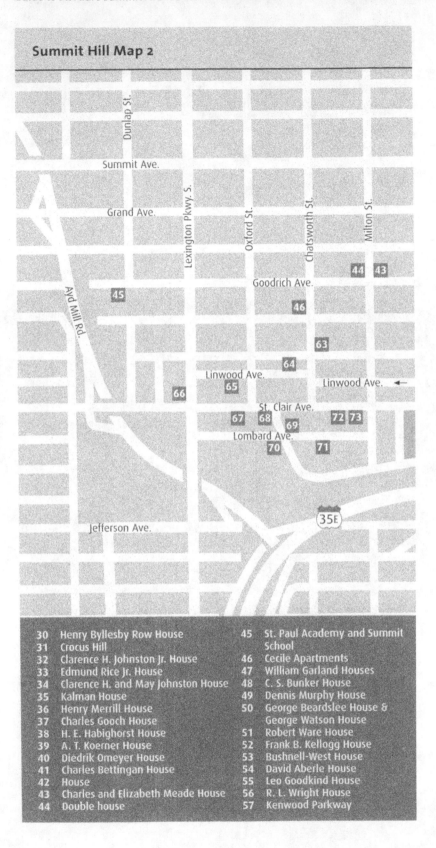

Summit Hill Map 2

30	Henry Byllesby Row House	45	St. Paul Academy and Summit
31	Crocus Hill		School
32	Clarence H. Johnston Jr. House	46	Cecile Apartments
33	Edmund Rice Jr. House	47	William Garland Houses
34	Clarence H. and May Johnston House	48	C. S. Bunker House
35	Kalman House	49	Dennis Murphy House
36	Henry Merrill House	50	George Beardslee House &
37	Charles Gooch House		George Watson House
38	H. E. Habighorst House	51	Robert Ware House
39	A. T. Koerner House	52	Frank B. Kellogg House
40	Diedrik Omeyer House	53	Bushnell-West House
41	Charles Bettingan House	54	David Aberle House
42	House	55	Leo Goodkind House
43	Charles and Elizabeth Meade House	56	R. L. Wright House
44	Double house	57	Kenwood Parkway

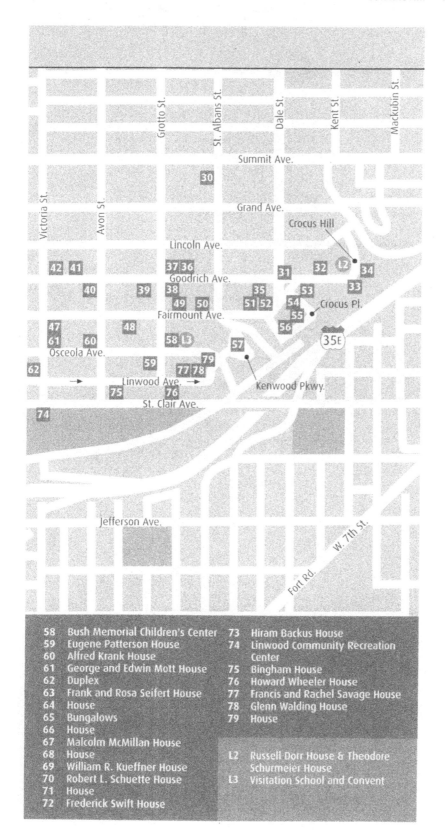

58	Bush Memorial Children's Center	73	Hiram Backus House
59	Eugene Patterson House	74	Linwood Community Recreation
60	Alfred Krank House		Center
61	George and Edwin Mott House	75	Bingham House
62	Duplex	76	Howard Wheeler House
63	Frank and Rosa Seifert House	77	Francis and Rachel Savage House
64	House	78	Glenn Walding House
65	Bungalows	79	House
66	House		
67	Malcolm McMillan House		
68	House	L2	Russell Dorr House & Theodore
69	William R. Kueffner House		Schurmeier House
70	Robert L. Schuette House	L3	Visitation School and Convent
71	House		
72	Frederick Swift House		

These were a stock item made by the Midland Terra Cotta Co. of Chicago, which offered a variety of Sullivanesque pieces in its catalog in the 1920s.

6 Grand Place

870 Grand Ave.

Pope Architects, 2001

A modern shopping complex, treated in the faux historical manner that has become more of an architectural curse than a blessing. A parking ramp hides behind the upper facades like a naughty child banished to his room.

Oxford Hill Condominiums and Shops

7 Oxford Hill Condominiums and Shops

1060 Grand Ave.

ESG Architects, 2005

Nostalgia in brick and cast-stone, though nicely done of its kind. There are 36 apartments above the ground-floor shops.

Lexington Restaurant

8 Lexington Restaurant

1096 Grand Ave.

1911 / renovated, Werner Wittkamp, ca. 1955

This old-line restaurant offers one of the avenue's liveliest facades, a collection of pediments, pilasters, cornices, arches, keystones, and shutters pasted like oversized Post-it notes to the smooth brick walls. Their message seems to be, "I've got class."

Maybe so, but the design's perilous proximity to pure fifties kitsch is what makes it so much fun. The man responsible for all the architectural mischief here was German-born Werner Wittkamp, who began his career as a set designer. He worked for the Ziegfeld Follies and on several Hollywood films before landing in St. Paul.

POI A Lincoln Court Apartments

93–95 Lexington Pkwy. South

J. Walter Stevens, 1921

This building is most notable for what happened in a third-floor hallway on March 31, 1934, when police and FBI agents arrived to investigate reports of a suspicious couple living in one of the apartments. The twosome turned out to be John Dillinger (using the evocative alias of Carl Hellman) and his companion, Evelyn Frechette. The lawmen's arrival touched off a furious gunfight. Despite the proverbial hail of bullets, Dillinger and Frechette somehow escaped and no one was hurt. Less than three months later, Dillinger was shot dead by FBI agents outside a Chicago movie theater.

The Dillinger shootout wasn't the only gangster-era crime in this neighborhood. Just two months earlier, on January 17, 1934, members of the Karpis-Barker gang kidnapped banker Edward Bremer, pulling him from his car at the corner of Lexington Pkwy. and Goodrich Ave. Bremer was held three weeks and then released after his family paid a $200,000 ransom.

9 William and Martha Horne House !

993 Lincoln Ave.

Allen H. Stem, 1889

Perhaps the most fetching Shingle Style house in the Twin Cities. Wrapped in a taut skin of dark shingles, the house's bays, projections, balconies, and curving corners enliven the overall design, as do windows of all shapes and sizes. The large bowed window to the right of the entry porch is especially fine (and, with 84 panes, no doubt a chore to clean). Note also the exquisite little

William and Martha Horne House

dormer roosting midway up the catslide roof over the entry porch. The home's first owner, William Horne, was vice president of Horne and Danz Co., a St. Paul firm that manufactured tinware.

10 House N

899 Lincoln Ave.

ca. 1910

The Spanish Mission Revival style, which summons up images of sun-kissed adobe walls and Zorro lurking in the shadows, found its way to the Twin Cities just after 1900. This broad brick house is a good local example of the style despite a tacky addition on the east side and other misadventures in remodeling. The dominant design element is a central dormer sculpted in the approved Mission manner and punctured by quatrefoil windows. A large garage on the property also sports a dormer as well as a superb brick arch above the doors.

11 House (Babies Home of St. Paul) N

846 Lincoln Ave.

1880

An unusually old house for this area and one with quite a history. In 1891 a group of women bought the property and turned it into the Babies Home of St. Paul, a refuge for impoverished, abandoned, and orphaned infants, of

which there was no shortage at the time. In its first four years of operation, the home accommodated nearly 300 infants, some of whom were eventually adopted or reclaimed by their parents. It's not known how long the Babies Home was here, but city directories indicate it was gone by no later than 1932.

Oliver and Elizabeth Crosby House

12 Oliver and Elizabeth Crosby House N

804 Lincoln Ave.

Clarence H. Johnston, 1900 and later

Oliver Crosby, an engineer and inventor who cofounded the American Hoist and Derrick Co. in St. Paul, is best remembered for Stonebridge, a later mansion he built along Mississippi River Blvd. in the Macalester-Groveland neighborhood. Still, this four-square stone house, newly restored, is impressive in its own right. Except for the lacy Gothic bargeboards decorating the attic dormers, the house isn't strongly styled. Instead, it conveys a sense of solid utilitarianism, undoubtedly part of what made it appealing to an engineer like Crosby.

13 John H. Bryant House N

776 Lincoln Ave.

ca. 1882 / later additions

One of the neighborhood's oldest homes, so extensively modified that only a few original features, such as its pedimented window hoods, can still be seen.

14 James Doran House N

745 Lincoln Ave.

Charles Bussford, 1904

A large brick house notable for its terra-cotta trim, which includes a decorative panel between two of the second-story windows.

Stickler Row

15 Stickler Row N

733–39 Lincoln Ave.

Charles A. Wallingford, 1890

This sandstone row house, marooned in Colonial Revival country, offers a lively alternative to its rather restrained neighbors. It comes with all the requisite Victorian goodies—bays, balconies, terraces, towers, carved decorative panels, and even a neat circular window thrown in for good measure. Despite all that's going on, the front facade is essentially symmetrical. A real estate developer named Augustus Wilgus built the row house and lived in one of the apartments.

16 Houses N

706, 710, 716 Lincoln Ave.

1908–10

Three brick beauties with broad front porches and fine detailing. The houses are Colonial Revival in character but quite free in their interpretation of the style. The most distinctive of the trio, at 716 Lincoln, features Roman brick, Tudor-arched windows on the upper stories, and much fine leaded and stained glass.

Ladislav Pavlicek House

17 Ladislav Pavlicek House N

567 Lincoln Ave.

1910

A mixed-style house with eccentric massing and a long front

gable that swoops down over the front door. The original owner, Ladislav Pavlicek, was an interior designer, which may explain the house's peculiarities.

Horace E. Stevens–Charles H. Bigelow Jr. House

18 Horace E. Stevens– Charles H. Bigelow Jr. House ! N L

530 Grand Hill

Reed and Stem, 1895 / addition, ca. 1923

This powerful red brick house, built for an engineer who obviously believed in the Victorian gospel of weight and mass, is among the most impressive of its time in the Twin Cities. Although its pointed-arch windows evoke Gothic Revival, the house has almost none of the applied ornament or busy surface texturing typical of the style. Instead, it reads as a dense, sculpted object into which windows seem to have been inserted with reluctance. The front porch, unique in St. Paul, is particularly striking, as are the chimneys that rise like pylons to either side. The architect, Allen Stem, is not so well known locally as Cass Gilbert or Clarence Johnston, but he was in their league. Charles Bigelow, Jr., president of the Farwell, Ozmun and Kirk (FOK) Hardware Co., bought the house in 1923 and built a large rear addition that nicely matches the original design.

Cass and Julia Gilbert House

19 Cass and Julia Gilbert House N L

1 Heather Pl.

Gilbert and Taylor, 1890 / altered, ca. 1923

Gilbert and his wife, Julia, lived here from 1890 until they moved to New York City in 1900. With its gables, bays, and porch, the house falls into the picturesque mode that Gilbert—despite his renown as a classicist—typically handled with considerable finesse. The house today does not look as it did when Gilbert designed it. In the 1920s an owner apparently infatuated with the then popular Tudor Revival style replaced the original shingle cladding above the first story with stucco and half-timbering. The interior also has been significantly modified.

20 Goodkind Double House ! N L

5–7 Heather Pl.

Reed and Stem, 1910

A giant double house, rendered as an exercise in pure English romance and occupying a gorgeous site atop the Grand Ave. hill. Sprawling across its wooded grounds, the house unfolds in a nostalgic panorama of limestone, stucco, and half-timbering beneath a wood shake roof that

curls around the eaves in imitation of thatch. The house is in a Tudor variant sometimes called the Cotswold Cottage style, although the term *cottage* seems a tad insufficient in this case.

It was built for brothers Benjamin and William Goodkind, both of whom were connected with the Mannheimer Brothers Department Store in downtown St. Paul. Benjamin was president of the firm, while William served as secretary and treasurer. Befitting his status, Benjamin lived in the larger of the two houses, at 7 Heather Pl. With about 8,500 square feet, it's nearly twice as large as the other side, 5 Heather Pl., where William resided. The only link between the houses is a bridgelike second-story passageway supported by heavy timbers and spanning a small central courtyard and fountain. The two sides of the property remain under separate ownership to this day.

The grounds, once about three acres but now reduced by subdivision, include a superb limestone retaining wall—quite possibly the longest on any residential property in the Twin Cities—that extends for hundreds of feet along Grand Ave. A second wall runs along the hillside above, and there's also a winding stone staircase (now closed) that leads up to the house from a gated entry on Grand. Unfortunately, the Goodkinds did not enjoy their estate for long. Both moved out by 1920, possibly because of financial reverses stemming from their failed attempt to build a new store in what later became the Hamm Building.

Summit Hill

Goodkind Double House

21 William J. Dean House N *L*

514 Grand Hill

Cass Gilbert, 1894

A carefully detailed Colonial Revival house, built for a partner in Nicols and Dean, a hardware wholesaling firm. In this same year Gilbert also designed a house on White Bear Lake for William B. Dean, father of William J.

Charles and Mary Ames House

22 Charles and Mary Ames House N *L*

501 Grand Hill

J. N. Tilton (Chicago), 1886

This exuberant, rambling Shingle Style home might be called the house of many gables. Six are visible from the street (one in front, two on the east side, three on the west), and others lurk to the rear. Little is known about the Chicago architect who designed the house other than that he seems to have dreaded the thought of a dull roofline. Charles Ames was secretary of West Publishing Co. when he and his wife, Mary, commissioned this house. Ames later became West's general manager. F. Scott Fitzgerald, a friend of Ames's son, Theodore, described the home's backyard in one of his Basil Duke Lee stories.

23 Carl Schuneman House N *L*

489 Grand Hill

Stem and Haslund, 1925

One of the more monumental houses on Grand Hill, featuring rugged limestone walls and cut stone trim. The house, Tudor Revival in style, was built for a member of the family that owned Schuneman's Department Store in St. Paul. It's possible the house

incorporates portions of an earlier mansion built in 1887.

Frederick Weyerhaeuser House

24 Frederick Weyerhaeuser House N *L*

480 Grand Hill

William Channing Whitney, 1908

A Tudor Revival mansion designed for the lumber king near the end of his life by Minneapolis society architect William Channing Whitney. Like much of Whitney's work, the house is well done but not especially lively. Incidentally, the short street now called Grand Hill used to be a part of Grand Ave., which was crossed by Oakland Ave. here as it descended the long hill toward West Seventh St. The lower part of Oakland (along the hill) was renamed Grand in 1970, while this portion of Grand became Grand Hill. Such confused street genealogy is typical of St. Paul.

25 Paul Gotzian House N *L*

33 Summit Ct. (also 32 Lawton St.)

Gilbert and Taylor, 1889 / enlarged and remodeled, Thomas Holyoke, 1903

A Gothic-tinged stone foursquare, similar to Gilbert's Dittenhofer House of 1898 at 705 Summit Ave.

26 Robert Bement House N *L*

27 Summit Ct.

Gilbert and Taylor, 1888

Another of Gilbert's forays into eclecticism. The porch columns have Medieval-inspired capitals, the corner tower evokes the Shingle Style, while the design as a whole appears to be moving toward Colonial Revival. Bement was a businessman with diverse interests who also served as president of the St. Paul Water Board in the 1890s.

27 George Squires House N *L*

19 Summit Ct.

Gilbert and Taylor, 1889

The type of symmetrical facades that Gilbert favored in the early 1890s first appeared on this house, built for a St. Paul attorney. It's one of at least nine houses Gilbert designed along Summit Ct., Heather Pl., and Grand Hill.

POI B Interstate 35E Parkway

Between Mississippi River and I-94

Minnesota Highway Department, 1956 and later

Construction of this interstate highway wiped out numerous homes and other buildings along the old Pleasant Ave. corridor. The freeway was supposed to have been opened in 1972 (planning actually began in the 1950s), but fierce neighborhood opposition delayed completion until 1989. The long battle was finally resolved by a series of compromises that make this one of the country's most unusual stretches of interstate highway. It has only four lanes, the speed limit is 45 miles an hour, and it's designated a "parkway" from which large trucks are banned. Trivia buffs may be interested to know that 35E is also one of only four interstate segments in the United States that still has a letter as part of its designation (the others are 35W in Minneapolis and a similar east-west divide as the freeway passes through Fort Worth and Dallas, TX).

POI C Lawton Street Steps and house

Steps, between Grand Ave. and Grand Hill

1911 / restored, St. Paul Department of Public Works, 1992

House, 70 Lawton St.

2004

These 78 steps connect Grand Ave. to Grand Hill. Midway up the stairs is a house accessible only on foot. It replaced an earlier home owned by Conrad O. Searle, a St. Paul architect.

Jared Howe House

28 Jared Howe House !

455 Grand Ave.

Louis Lockwood, 1907

Located next to the Lawton St. steps, this one-of-a-kind house features an unusual two-story front porch supported by stone and brick piers, a hipped roof over bracketed eaves, and a covered side entry with bottle-glass windows. Figuring out the house's style—which stirs Gothic, Classical, Arts and Crafts, and even Japanese-inspired elements into the mix—is no simple matter. Its closest architectural relatives appear to be colonial-era bungalows built by the British in India. Architect Louis Lockwood, born and trained in England, would have been familiar with the British bungalow style. Jared Howe, the first owner, was a partner in the prestigious St. Paul law firm of Howe, Butler and Mitchell. He was also a bachelor, which may explain why the house's interior has something of the feel of a private gentlemen's club. In addition to the house, which is now a duplex, the property includes the original garage.

29 Apartments N

587 Grand Ave.

1925

Of the many vintage walk-up apartment buildings on Grand, this one has perhaps the most elaborate facade, a Renaissance Revival stage set that includes a pair of blind arches infilled with brick in a herringbone pattern

587 Grand Ave.

to either side of the front door. Plaques and other ornamental features complete the decorative ensemble.

Henry Byllesby Row House

30 Henry Byllesby Row House N

21–27 South St. Albans St.

Clarence H. Johnston, 1892

A fine piece of Victorian street theater, named after the businessman who built it. The facades of each of the four units are treated differently but still combine to form a convincing whole. The row house is one of Clarence Johnston's first forays into the Tudor Revival variant known as Jacobethan, although there are Romanesque Revival elements as well.

31 Crocus Hill

Goodrich Ave. east of Dale St.

The block-long, blufftop street known as Crocus Hill has a peculiar house numbering system, even by St. Paul standards. Originally the houses were numbered in order of construction, with 1 Crocus Hill being the oldest and so on. However, since many of the homes here are second generation, the numbering system's link to chronology has grown tenuous.

32 Clarence H. Johnston Jr. House N

11 Crocus Hill

1887 / remodeled, Clarence H. Johnston, Jr., 1912

Like his father, Clarence Johnston, Jr., was an architect, and this pleasing Arts and Craftsy house is one of his most successful creations.

Edmund Rice Jr. House

33 Edmund Rice Jr. House N

4 Crocus Hill

William Channing Whitney, 1886 / later remodelings

The street's oldest, largest, and most indisputably romantic house, situated at the end of Crocus Hill on a lot that commands a sweeping view of the river valley. Its original owner was Edmund Rice, Jr., a real estate agent who never lived here. The tower that rises above the layered roofline is a modern addition, and many changes were also made to the house in the 1920s.

34 Clarence H. and May Johnston House N

2 Crocus Hill

1884 / rebuilt, Clarence H. Johnston, 1909

The architect's own house and, like the man, rather unassuming. Johnston lived here until his death in 1936.

Russell Dorr House, 1888

LOST 2 *Two spectacular Victorian mansions, the **Russell Dorr House***

*(at 5 Crocus Hill) and the **Theodore Schurmeier House** (6 Crocus Hill), once stood nearby. Both were designed by Clarence Johnston (with William Willcox) in 1887. Neither managed to outlive their architect, however, with the Schurmeier house coming down just a year before Johnston died.*

35 Kalman House

626 Goodrich Ave.

1892

A colorful Queen Anne with a tall round tower topped by a bulbous roof from which four bull's-eye windows peep out at the world. F. Scott and Zelda Fitzgerald lived here with their baby daughter, Scottie, in 1921–22.

36 Henry Merrill House N

707 Goodrich Ave.

J. Walter Stevens, 1901

One of the neighborhood's more monumental Colonial Revival houses, although the front facade looks rather cramped because the windows are so close together.

37 Charles Gooch House N

725 Goodrich Ave.

Clarence H. Johnston, 1902

There are traces of the Colonial Revival, Chateauesque, and Tudor Revival styles in this yellow brick house, which despite its eclecticism still comes across as a convincing design.

38 H. E. Habighorst House N

736 Goodrich Ave.

Augustus Gauger, 1896 / later remodelings

A Queen Anne–Colonial Revival hybrid that sports a round corner tower topped by a witch's-hat roof.

39 A. T. Koerner House N

748 Goodrich Ave.

ca. 1885 / later remodelings

One of the oldest houses in the neighborhood. The shingled front gables appear to be a modern reconstruction.

Diedrik Omeyer House

40 Diedrik Omeyer House N

808 Goodrich Ave.

Omeyer and Thori, 1889 / restored, Hengelfelt Restorations, 2004

Oh, those crazy Norwegians! The duo of Omeyer and Thori specialized in mad-dog Victorian houses, foaming with ornament. This is one of their prime extravaganzas, and it will clear your sinuses just by looking at it. The house was originally owned by architect Diedrik Omeyer, who with his partner in excess, Martin Thori, left fingerprints on gaudy Queen Anne houses all around St. Paul. For many years, this architectural wild thing was tamed by modern siding, but a restoration in 2004 brought it back to vibrant life. The restored front porch is especially fine.

41 Charles Bettingan House N

825 Goodrich Ave.

Louis Lockwood, 1900

A house that rambles all over its large lot but never settles on any particular style, displaying a free mix of Tudor, Colonial Revival, and Shingle Style elements. The pivot point is a portly corner tower topped by a finial that seems to erupt out of a giant swirl of whipped cream. The first owner, Charles Bettingan, was an executive for a plumbing supply company.

42 House N

833 Goodrich Ave.

Augustus Gauger, 1891

A late Victorian house with tall, richly textured front gables divided into three layers. Christopher C. Andrews, who pioneered modern forestry practices in Minnesota (a state forest bears his name), once owned this home.

Charles and Elizabeth Meade House

43 Charles and Elizabeth Meade House N

917 Goodrich Ave.

Mark Fitzpatrick, 1909

Instead of offering yet another take on Colonial Revival, architect Mark Fitzpatrick here found inspiration closer to home—in the work of Chicago architects Louis Sullivan and George Maher. The octagonal columns on the porch and the small niche above are in the manner of Sullivan, as are the squared-off, ornately carved capitals. But the house's broad proportions, widely spaced windows, and curious arched dormer show an even stronger affinity to homes designed by Maher in the early 1900s. Maher himself was no stranger to Minnesota, designing several important buildings in Winona as well as a mansion in the Lowry Hill neighborhood of Minneapolis. Little is known about the original owners of this house other than that Charles Meade was a physician.

44 Double house

921–25 Goodrich Ave.

1905

It's probably no coincidence that this house, which also has Sullivanesque features, stands directly across Milton St. from the Meade House, built four years later, though no obvious connection between the two is known. Here, however, the basic design is Colonial Revival and only the distinctive ornament around the second-story and dormer windows suggests Sullivan's influence.

45 St. Paul Academy and Summit School (Lower School)

1150 Goodrich Ave.

Clarence H. Johnston, 1924 / additions, 1951, 1958, 1963, and later

A Collegiate Gothic building, originally built for the Summit School for Girls, which in 1969 merged with the St. Paul Academy.

46 Cecile Apartments

145 South Chatsworth St.

1922

A good example of the center-court apartment buildings popular in the 1920s.

47 William Garland Houses N

846, 854–56 Fairmount Ave.

Omeyer and Thori, 1890

Here, St. Paul's principal providers of visual mayhem offer two more monuments to the art of the lathe and the jigsaw. The porches are particularly ornate. William Garland, a trunk manufacturer, is listed as the original owner of both houses, in which other members of his family also lived at various times.

48 C. S. Bunker House N

776 Fairmount Ave.

Walter Ife, 1894

Fairly routine Colonial Revival except for a delightful, child-sized porch inserted into the front gable. Ife was one of a number of English-born architects who worked in St. Paul in the 1880s and 1890s.

49 Dennis Murphy House N

731 Fairmount Ave.

Clarence H. Johnston, 1899

A very crisp Tudor Revival house with twin side gables, bargeboards, and a tall chimney laid up in brick of varying colors.

George Beardslee (left) & George Watson Houses

50 George Beardslee House N

703 Fairmount Ave.

Willcox and Johnston, 1889

George Watson House N

701 Fairmount Ave.

Willcox and Johnston, 1889

A pair of houses by the same architects that show how readily the Shingle and Colonial Revival styles could be scrambled together in the late 1880s.

51 Robert Ware House N

645 Fairmount Ave.

J. Walter Stevens, 1900

An unusually elaborate dormer rises from the center of this oddly proportioned house, which has a corner tower that seems to throw the whole design off kilter.

Frank B. Kellogg House

52 Frank B. Kellogg House ! N L

633 Fairmount Ave.

William H. Willcox, 1890 / addition, Allen H. Stem, 1923

Although Frank Kellogg is not well remembered today, except perhaps as the namesake of Kellogg Blvd. in St. Paul, he was known around the world in the 1920s for negotiating the Kellogg-Briand Pact, an agreement in which over 60 nations renounced war (but not for long). Kellogg, who served as secretary of state under President Calvin Coolidge, won the Nobel Prize for Peace in 1930 for his efforts. Before moving onto the international stage, he was a highly successful attorney in St. Paul and Minnesota's first popularly elected U.S. senator.

His stone- and shingle-clad house, designated a National Historic Landmark in 1976, is as interesting for its architecture as for its history. The main part of the house, completed in 1890, was designed by William Willcox in a convincing amalgam of the Richardsonian Romanesque and Shingle styles. A brawny tower, built largely of pink quartzite from southwestern Minnesota, dominates the south side. To the east, overlooking the garden, the house is less forbidding, with a double gable rising above an inset arcade. In 1923 a large addition was constructed on the northeast side of the house, where the front entrance is now located. The addition became known as the "Coolidge Wing" after a visit from Silent Cal himself. Kellogg lived here until his death in 1937.

Bushnell-West House

53 Bushnell-West House N

91 Crocus Pl.

Charles E. Joy, 1888

A house with some wonderfully weird features, among them a curving second-floor balcony that looks to be accessible only through a window and a stacked pair of dormers that appear poised to play a game of leapfrog across the roof. Why is it that no one ever seems to have had quite as much fun creating houses as the supposedly repressed Victorians?

David Aberle House

54 David Aberle House ! N

54 Crocus Pl.

Edwin Lundie, 1927

Architect Edwin Lundie worked in the offices of Cass Gilbert and Emmanuel Masqueray before striking off on his own in about 1920. Over the next 50 years he designed a series of exquisite houses in the Twin Cities and elsewhere in Minnesota, as well as a remarkable group of cabins and resort buildings along the north shore of Lake Superior. This house is one of Lundie's finest, done in the Cotswold Cottage variant of Tudor. It has beautifully laid-up walls of multi-colored limestone, a slate roof, and a pinwheeling floorplan designed to capture the site's views. As with all of Lundie's work, the details—note, for example the triangular fragments of slate shingles inserted at the corners of many of the eaves—are divine.

55 Leo Goodkind House N

40 Crocus Pl.

Allen H. Stem, 1914

Another Tudor mansion designed by Stem for a member of the Goodkind family. This one isn't as spectacular as the double house at 5–7 Heather Pl.; even so, the house is certainly impressive, with steep half-timbered gables rising above a limestone base.

56 R. L. Wright House N

30 Crocus Pl.

Reed and Stem, 1899

A Renaissance Revival–style brick box that could easily pass for an apartment or club building. Note how the pilasters seem to act like support columns for the thick band of bricks between the second and third floors. The house's multi-colored and -patterned brickwork is also unusual. The wrought-iron entrance porch is a modern addition.

Philip McQuinlan House

57 Kenwood Parkway N

Near South St. Albans St. and Osceola Ave.

This street, which forms a loop at the top of the bluffs, is one of the few in St. Paul with gateposts (don't worry: there are no guards, and the street is public). Among the fine homes here is the **Philip McQuinlan House** (26 Kenwood Pkwy.), a Maheresque design from 1914.

58 Bush Memorial Children's Center N

180 South Grotto St.

1971

Low brick buildings with shed roofs give a quiet residential feel to this children's group home.

LOST 3 From 1913 to 1966 this was the site of Visitation School and Convent, now located in Mendota Heights. Most of the brick walls here were originally part of the Visitation complex.

Eugene Patterson House

59 Eugene Patterson House N

744 Osceola Ave.

Thomas Holyoke, 1912

One of the neighborhood's more unusual and impressive homes, built of randomly laid blocks of yellow limestone. With its wide eaves and low-pitched roof, the house has the relaxed feel of an Italian villa, although its sturdy forms and bold but simple detailing also show the influence of the Arts and Crafts movement. The small, off-center balcony over the front entrance is enchanting. The original owner was the vice president of a mortgage company.

60 Alfred Krank House N

803 Osceola Ave.

Augustus Gauger, 1906

A big house with walls of rough-faced limestone, done in the Jacobean mode of Tudor Revival. Krank founded a St. Paul firm that manufactured cosmetics, shampoos, and related products. In 1926 he built a splendid new factory at 1885 University Ave.,

and that building (now known as Iris Park Place) is listed on the National Register of Historic Places. Just two years after the factory was completed, Krank died in an automobile accident when his car struck a trolley.

61 George and Edwin Mott House N

859 Osceola Ave.

1905

This duplex built for two brothers looks to have begun its life as a straightforward Classical Revival house with a columned, two-story front porch. But somewhere along the line the entire house was encased in rough stucco, while the porches received intricate cast-iron railings. The result is a home that looks like nothing else in the vicinity.

62 Duplex

863–65 Linwood Ave.

William F. Keefe, 1922

A Craftsman duplex with Prairie detailing in the windows. Keefe built a similar duplex at 1205 Summit Ave., also in 1922.

Frank and Rosa Seifert House

63 Frank and Rosa Seifert House !

975 Osceola Ave.

Bentley and Hausler, 1914

One of St. Paul's largest and finest Prairie Style houses, abounding in leaded glass and other ornamental touches. Although not as dynamic as Frank Lloyd Wright's best Prairie designs, it's a strong and knowing work by a pair of gifted architects. Clad in tapestry brick and stucco, the house is a two-story cube with one-story projecting volumes that include porches on the south and west sides and a polygonal window bay in between. There's also a second-story sleeping porch to the rear. In contrast to the irregular first floor, the second story is symmetrical, with windows either centered or paired at the corners. Unfortunately, the eaves have been altered and don't extend out as far as they once did. Note also the garage, designed to complement the house, and the large planter—a favorite Prairie School device—at the corner of the lot.

Little is known about the original owners other than that Frank Seifert apparently operated a billiard parlor in downtown St. Paul and seems to have been blessed with exceptionally advanced architectural tastes. The duo of Bentley and Hausler went on to design one other Prairie house in St. Paul, at 1599 Portland Ave., in 1915. After that, Hausler served a stint as St. Paul city architect while Bentley returned to his native city of La Crosse, WI, where he practiced until the 1930s.

64 House

995 Linwood Ave.

1892

Proof that just because a Victorian house is small doesn't mean it can't be very busy. This one has gables galore despite its modest dimensions.

65 Bungalows

1042–80 Linwood Ave.

T. L. Blood and other builders, ca. 1908–11

Here between Lexington Pkwy. and Oxford St. is St. Paul's finest collection of small bungalows, the bulk of which were built around 1910. What makes these homes so appealing is the quality of their detailing: many have half-timbering, some sport bargeboards, and leaded-glass windows are also common.

66 House

235 Lexington Pkwy. South

C. E. Peterson, 1922

A sophisticated Craftsman house, one of many of its kind in the vicinity.

67 Malcolm McMillan House

1058 St. Clair Ave.

Ernest Hartford and Charles A. Hausler, 1915

This house is basically a Craftsman stucco box, but the side entry, the piers that project to either side of the front windows, and the applied bands of wood on the second story are all features you might expect to find on a high-style Prairie house.

68 House

1028 St. Clair Ave.

1925

A Mission Revival bungalow—not a common sight in St. Paul.

69 William R. Kueffner House

10 Benhill Rd.

Clarence H. Johnston, 1915

Clarence Johnston designed four houses on Benhill Rd. between 1915 and 1925. This one, which is hard to see through the trees, has a casual, Arts and Crafts feel.

Linwood Ave. bungalows

70 Robert L. Schuette House

15 Benhill Rd.

Clarence H. Johnston, 1918

A large stone-clad house of no strong style. In the summer, a small artificial stream tumbles down a hill in the front yard.

970 Lombard Ave.

71 House

970 Lombard Ave.

1948

A one-story modernist house behind an intimate courtyard.

Frederick Swift House

72 Frederick Swift House

962 St. Clair Ave.

John Coxhead, 1888

Architect John Coxhead practiced in St. Paul for only five years, beginning in 1887, and many of his works are gone. But most of what survives, like this frothy Queen Anne concoction, is choice. An elaborate paint job highlights the house's amazing variety of textures, forms, and materials, although some decorative elements are presumably modern reconstructions.

73 Hiram Backus House

956 St. Clair Ave.

1890

A towered Victorian that's been covered in stucco—it's sort of like looking at a shaggy dog that's lost all of its hair. The original owner was one of the first managers of the Hotel Barteau (gone) in downtown St. Paul.

74 Linwood Community Recreation Center

860 St. Clair Ave.

1991

An ambitious attempt to re-create the presence of a towered, Victorian-era building on a steeply sloping site in Linwood Park. Unfortunately, the quality of today's materials isn't up to the standards of old, and the building isn't especially convincing.

75 Bingham House N

784 Linwood Ave.

James E. Niemeyer, 1927

The revival style du jour here is French Provincial. The white shutters add a quaint Storybook touch to the design.

Howard Wheeler House

76 Howard Wheeler House N

226 South Grotto St.

John W. Wheeler, 1905

A very large brick and stone house, done up in the grand Beaux-Arts manner that, in St. Paul, was usually reserved for mansions on or very close to Summit Ave. It's likely that architect John Wheeler, best known for his work at St. Catherine University a few miles to the west, was related to the lawyer who built this house.

77 Francis and Rachel Savage House N

719 Linwood Ave.

Peter J. Linhoff, 1915

A stately Georgian Revival house built for a doctor and his wife. It would look right at home on

Summit Ave., where Linhoff in fact designed over 15 residences.

Glenn Walding House

78 Glenn Walding House N

709 Linwood Ave.

James E. Niemeyer, 1916

A severely plain house that must have seemed ultramodern when it was built. The Craftsman-Prairie mix here is stripped down to bare essentials: with some rejiggering of proportions and other adjustments, this house could pass as a precursor of the International Style to come. Walding was secretary of the St. Paul Mutual Hail and Cyclone Insurance Co., and perhaps he wanted a compact, unadorned house so as to present the smallest possible target to either form of disaster.

79 House N

685 Linwood Ave.

1927

A romantic stone and stucco house, more French Provincial than anything, although the picturesque massing also calls to mind the English "cottage" style.

Summit-University West and North

There are two distinct urban environments here, separated by the chasm of Interstate 94, and only the area south of the freeway has retained a significant amount of its historic architectural character. North of the freeway, where Summit-University's official boundaries extend to University Avenue, wholesale urban renewal occurred in the 1950s and 1960s in what was known as the Western Redevelopment Area. Entire blocks were cleared and rebuilt in accord with the standard "suburbanized" model of the era, which specified large swaths of passive green space, cul-de-sacs rather than through streets, and midblock pedestrian pathways. The results weren't terrible, but the area now seems a world apart from the Hill District.

Extensive urban renewal also occurred in the blocks immediately south of the interstate, but farther down along Dayton, Hague, Laurel, Ashland, and Portland avenues hundreds of late nineteenth- and early twentieth-century homes still remain. These houses often lack the spit and polish of the Hill District's restored Victorians, but many are nonetheless of high architectural quality. Apartments, schools, churches, and commercial buildings (mainly along Selby Avenue) are also part of the mix.

There are no overwhelming architectural monuments in this part of Summit-University, but you will find houses designed by Clarence Johnston, Emmanuel Masqueray, Louis Lockwood, and Omeyer and Thori, among other prominent St. Paul architects. The homes here generally aren't as big as those farther east, but a few, such as the Susan Welch House (1894), qualify as mini-mansions. At the western edge of the neighborhood, on Lexington Parkway, is one of the city's most spectacular bungalows: the Stuart Cameron House (1911).

Here, too, at 901 Portland Ave., you'll find a charming English Gothic–style church, St. Clement's Episcopal (1895), designed by Cass Gilbert. Nearby on Portland is the old First Methodist Episcopal Church (1910), a Classical Revival–style building recently converted into a handsome new home for the SteppingStone Theatre.

1 Academy Professional Building (St. Paul Academy)

25 North Dale St.

Thomas Holyoke, 1903 / addition, ca. 1960 / renovated, Ed Conley, 2006 / Art: F. Scott Fitzgerald (statue), Aaron Dysart, 2006

F. Scott Fitzgerald attended school in this unremarkable building from 1908 to 1911, when it served as St. Paul Academy, then a private school for boys. The academy moved elsewhere in 1931, and the old school had a variety of occupants before it was converted to professional offices. A statue of Fitzgerald as a boy was placed on the building's front steps in 2006.

2 Condominiums (St. Paul Academy)

718–26 Portland Ave.

Magnus Jemne, 1931 / renovated, ca. 1980s

This was the Junior School of St. Paul Academy before being turned into condominiums in the 1980s. Magnus Jemne designed it—in a subdued version of the Moderne phase of art deco—not long after completing his sleek Women's City Club in downtown St. Paul. The building bears an uncanny resemblance to a number of public housing projects from the 1930s.

819 (right) and 823 Portland Ave.

3 Houses N *L*

819, 823, 829 Portland Ave.

Omeyer and Thori, 1889

Three brick Queen Annes that anchor the middle of a block. The star of the trio is the middle house at 823 Portland. It's unusual by virtue of its two towers, the shorter and stouter of which looks more like something from the Romanesque Revival than the Queen Anne. The iron fence in front of the house is modern; it was made in Scotland and installed in 2005.

4 SteppingStone Theatre (First Methodist Episcopal Church) N *L*

873 Portland Ave. (also 55 North Victoria St).

Thori, Alban and Fischer, 1910 / renovated, Duan Corp. (Frank Duan), 2007

This updated version of a Roman temple, mounted on a high basement, is a rarity in the Twin Cities due to both its style and its size. The colossal Ionic portico makes a big architectural statement and also forms a terminal vista at the

end of Holly Ave. Beyond its impressive portico, the church is a very simple design, with rows of regularly spaced windows marching along its side walls. First Methodist remained in the building until 1959. Two other congregations later occupied the church, which in 2007 was renovated to become the Stepping-Stone Theatre's new home. The old sanctuary was converted into a 430-seat proscenium-arch theater, and there are also classrooms and administrative offices.

St. Clement's Episcopal Church

5 St. Clement's Episcopal Church ! N *L*

901 Portland Ave.

Cass Gilbert, 1895 / addition, Clarence H. Johnston, 1913

A lovely work by Cass Gilbert modeled on an English parish church. The Gothic elements are carried out very simply, with buttressed walls of yellow limestone supporting a steeply gabled roof punctuated by six delicate dormers. Rising from one side is a finely proportioned bell tower that

SteppingStone Theatre

Summit-University West and North

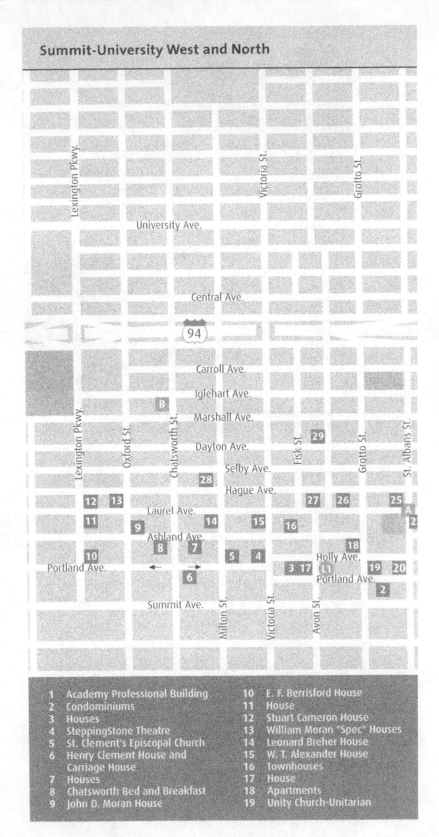

1	Academy Professional Building	10	E. F. Berrisford House
2	Condominiums	11	House
3	Houses	12	Stuart Cameron House
4	SteppingStone Theatre	13	William Moran "Spec" Houses
5	St. Clement's Episcopal Church	14	Leonard Breher House
6	Henry Clement House and Carriage House	15	W. T. Alexander House
		16	Townhouses
7	Houses	17	House
8	Chatsworth Bed and Breakfast	18	Apartments
9	John D. Moran House	19	Unity Church-Unitarian

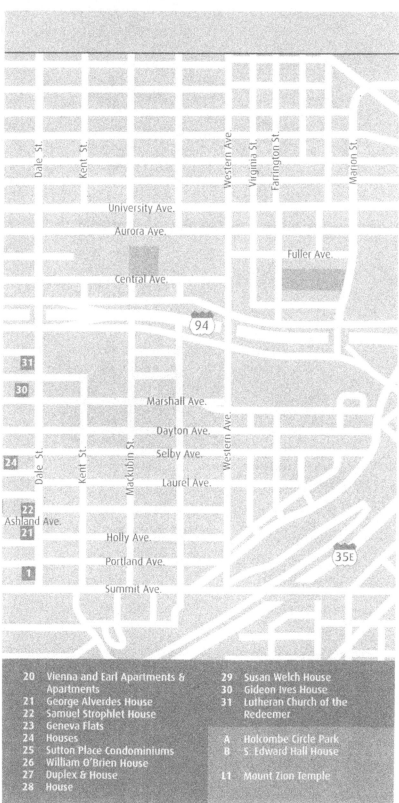

culminates in a stone spire. The grounds include a lych-gate—an entry gate with benches to either side that is often part of English country churchyards. The intimate worship space within features a hammer-beam ceiling, brilliantly colored stencilwork, an oak rood screen, and Tiffany glass. Gilbert himself is said to have painted some of the decorations around the altar; he later complained bitterly when parts of the church were, in his words, "marred by other hands."

The church was built with a $25,000 gift from Mrs. Theodore Eaton of New York. Her husband had been rector of St. Clement's Church there, and this church was given the same name in his honor. The dedication on October 6, 1895, was an impressive affair that attracted such eastern society elites as Mrs. J. P. Morgan (one source says the great financier himself also attended). A parish hall and a vestibule were added in 1913, but the historic church proper remains largely as built.

6 Henry Clement House and Carriage House N L

948 Portland Ave.

Peter J. Linhoff, 1908

A handsome brick home with its original carriage house still intact. The house convincingly applies Tudor Revival details, such as a gable with bargeboards, to what is basically an American foursquare format.

7 House

950–52 Ashland Ave.

Omeyer and Thori?, 1891

House

957 Ashland Ave.

Omeyer and Thori?, 1889

These two restored Victorians, neither of which can be accused of excessive restraint, are a decade or so older than most of the other houses on this block. They look to be from the Omeyer and Thori collection of Queen Annes, although city building records don't list an architect for either house.

8 Chatsworth Bed and Breakfast (Henry Wessel House)

984 Ashland Ave.

Louis Lockwood, 1900

Another unusual variation on the Colonial Revival from Lockwood. The most distinctive feature here is the full-length porch, which has limestone corner piers, a solid limestone balustrade, and four Ionic columns with brackets and oval medallions above the capitals. Lockwood also designed the striking Colonial Revival house just a few doors down at 993 Ashland.

John D. Moran House

9 John D. Moran House

1039 Ashland Ave.

Emmanuel Masqueray, 1909

This foursquare isn't as grand as the other Masqueray-designed house in St. Paul at 427 Portland Ave., but it's unmistakably different from anything else in this neighborhood. The handling of the brickwork, particularly on the second story, and the design of the front porch are unusual, and the house conveys a stately Beaux-Arts sensibility despite its modest size. The original owner, John D. Moran, ran a railroad construction company in St. Paul and was a friend of Archbishop John Ireland. That connection probably led Moran to choose Masqueray as his architect. The house fell vacant in the 1980s and was boarded up before being rescued by new owners, who lovingly restored it.

10 E. F. Berrisford House N L

1089 Portland Ave.

Edward J. Donahue, 1906

A large brick Colonial Revival house, very imposing on its corner lot. It has a number of curious Sullivanesque touches, such as the small second-story window that's set within a heavy stone frame.

11 House

116 Lexington Pkwy. North

ca. 1915

A good medium-sized example of the formal, boxy variation of the Prairie Style favored by Chicago architect George Maher. A number of these "Maheresque" houses, generally built between 1910 and 1920, are scattered throughout the Twin Cities.

12 Stuart Cameron House

130 Lexington Pkwy. North

Alban and Hausler, 1911

A show-stopping Craftsman bungalow with just a hint of Swiss Chalet styling thrown in for good measure. The broad roof has a single half-timbered dormer and shelters a long porch with brick piers and tall wood-slat balustrades. Bargeboards, exposed rafters, acorn pendants, and leaded-glass windows are among the house's many fine details. It was built for the superintendent of an ironworks company in St. Paul.

1050 Hague Ave.

13 William Moran "Spec" Houses

1048, 1050 Hague Ave.

William H. Castner, 1890

Two marvelous Shingle Style houses built on speculation. The house at 1048 Hague is full of inventive details, including a polygonal tower that ties into a balcony nestled beneath a gable with flared eaves. The east side of the house offers an eccentric array of windows, some of them tiny, that cut into or project out from the shingled walls. The house at 1050 Hague is quite different, with a long roof that sweeps down over a corner entry porch, but it's just as enchanting as its neighbor. Very little is known about architect William Castner other than that he began to specialize in Shingle Style designs in the late 1880s.

14 Leonard Breher House

928 Laurel Ave.

William Linley Alban, 1909

A house that manages to wring something fresh and engaging

Stuart Cameron House

out of the overworked Colonial Revival idiom. Small things make this design sing: the way the capitals of the paired Ionic porch columns curl up into brackets, the subtle flaring lines of the roof and gable, and, most of all, the swan's-neck pediment that sits atop the small second-story window like a party hat. William Alban, a largely forgotten St. Paul architect, worked skillfully in a variety of early twentieth-century styles.

15 W. T. Alexander House

876 Laurel Ave.

Omeyer and Thori, 1889

Another insanely festive house from St. Paul's Queen Anne wild men.

16 Townhouses

825–31 Ashland Ave.

1982

Boldly scaled glassed-in porches distinguish these infill townhouses.

17 House

806–8 Holly Ave.

1890

A finely restored house caught somewhere between the Shingle and Colonial Revival styles, with a dollop of Queen Anne thrown in as well. Such mixed-pedigree houses are far more common than the "pure" examples that usually show up in architectural textbooks.

Mount Zion Temple, 1935

LOST 1 *A parking lot at the southeast corner of Holly Ave. and Avon St. was once the site of Mount Zion Temple. Built in 1904 and demolished in about 1970, the synagogue was one of Clarence Johnston's outstanding designs, with a central dome rising above a porticoed temple front. The Mount Zion congregation vacated the building in the 1950s after completing a new temple on Summit Ave.*

744 Ashland Ave.

18 Apartments (Temple of Aaron and Jewish Educational Center)

744 Ashland Ave. and 741–59 Holly Ave.

Allen H. Stem (synagogue), 1916 / renovated after fire, 1952 / Liebenberg and Kaplan (educational center), 1930

These buildings, now apartments, originally served as a synagogue and educational complex for the Temple of Aaron, one of the city's prominent Jewish congregations. The synagogue on Ashland combines Byzantine and Romanesque elements in a way intended to set it apart from contemporaneous Christian churches. There's little decoration other than a Star of David and Torah tablets above the entrance. The educational center on Holly was one of the first Moderne-style buildings designed by Liebenberg and Kaplan, best known for their many theaters in the Twin Cities. Temple of Aaron relocated to a new synagogue on Mississippi River Blvd. in 1957, after which Beth Israel Temple moved in for about 20 years.

19 Unity Church-Unitarian

732 Holly Ave. (also 739 Portland Ave.)

Thomas Holyoke, 1905 / addition, Holyoke Jemne and Davis, 1921 / rebuilt after fire, HGA, 1964

This is St. Paul's only Unitarian church, founded in 1872. The church complex is something of a hodgepodge, but a comfortable one, reflecting both changing styles of architecture and the changing needs of the congregation. The oldest part is the church

Unity Church-Unitarian

proper, a pleasant stone building, Medieval in character. It includes a beguiling, perfectly scaled bell tower topped by a polygonal spire. A variety of additions, the earliest of which dates to 1921, have nearly surrounded the original church but on the whole do so respectfully. The original sanctuary was extensively remodeled after a 1963 fire; the courtyard and new entrance on the west side of the church were also added at that time.

Vienna and Earl Apartments

20 Vienna and Earl Apartments N L

682–88 Holly Ave.

Louis Lockwood, 1907

Apartments (boiler house)

47 North St. Albans St.

Louis Lockwood, 1907 / renovated, ca. 1982

These brick and concrete apartment buildings, luxurious in their day, are among the last works of the prolific St. Paul architect Louis Lockwood, who died in 1907 at age 43. Each building features six 1,300-square-foot apartments elegantly finished in oak. They were constructed for Carl P.

Waldon, a Swedish immigrant who started out as a bricklayer but later became a contractor and developer. From the early 1890s until his death in 1910, Waldon built or developed numerous apartment buildings in St. Paul, including the San Mateo Flats on Laurel Ave., where F. Scott Fitzgerald was born. To the rear of the apartments is a boiler house that once provided power to both buildings. In the 1980s it was converted into apartments after being "Victorianized" with the addition of dormers, window hoods, and various ornamental features.

George Alverdes House

21 George Alverdes House

633 Holly Ave.

Hausler and Wright, 1919

A late Prairie Style house by Charles A. Hausler and one of the many partners he teamed up with over the years, Myrtus Wright. The house has a long one-story "prow" extending out from a two-story block that features a front bay with angled windows; a shorter one-story section is on the other side. As is typical of Prairie houses, the front door, located behind a small porch, does not directly face the street. Because it was built on a modest budget of $5,000, the house lacks the exquisite ornamental detail, especially art glass, found in many Prairie designs. The original owner, George Alverdes, was the proprietor of a popular St. Paul restaurant that bore his name.

22 Samuel Strophlet House

633 Ashland Ave.

J. H. Strophlet (Pittsburgh), 1884

A sweet little cottage with unusual ornamental panels featuring inset circles. Built on Ninth St. in downtown St. Paul, it was moved here a short time later by its first owner, Samuel Strophlet. The architect of record, J. H. Strophlet, was undoubtedly a relative, since this is hardly the sort of commission that would normally have attracted a designer all the way from Pittsburgh.

23 Geneva Flats

110 North St. Albans St.

Charles A. Wallingford, 1892

A crisp apartment building with a stone base and oriel windows on the second floor. Wallingford designed several other apartment buildings in or near the Historic Hill District.

POI A Holcombe Circle Park

Laurel Ave. and St. Albans St.

1857

One of the neighborhood's curiosities, this tiny plot of greenery was dedicated in 1857 as a "market square," although a hot dog stand is about all that would fit here. It's named after William Holcombe, Minnesota's first lieutenant governor and, like almost everyone else in those pioneer days, a real estate speculator.

24 Houses

659, 661, 667 Hague Ave.

ca. 1880–85

Three "cottages" that show you don't need towers, elaborate porches, or great gobs of gingerbread to have a charming Victorian house.

25 Sutton Place Condominiums (Gilman Terrace)

697–703 Laurel Ave.

Hermann Kretz, 1892

This vivid Victorian is one of the neighborhood's architectural highlights, although it's only about half the building it used to be. Its western portion, where there's now a parking lot, was lopped off in the early 1930s for reasons unknown. Still, what remains is impressive. Clad in deep red brick above a brown-

stone base, the building has two ornate wooden porches, balconies with iron railings, and checkerboard patterning beneath some

Sutton Place Condominiums

windows. Unfortunately, those windows are now of the single-pane modern variety, whereas the originals were all double-hung, some with stained-glass transoms. Architect Hermann Kretz was responsible for several large St. Paul apartment buildings of this period, including the Blair House nearby at Selby and Western Aves.

William O'Brien House

26 William O'Brien House

765 Laurel Ave.

1884 / additions, 1891 and later

Maybe the smallest house in St. Paul with two front porches. The one on the east appears to be original (if modified), but the other is a modern addition.

27 Duplex

800 Hague Ave.

Omeyer and Thori, 1889

House

796 Hague Ave.

Omeyer and Thori, 1891

A pair of snazzy Queen Annes from the Omeyer and Thori design factory. The house at 796 Hague has exceptional stained-glass transoms above its two largest windows. The duplex at 800 Hague features a pedimented central gable and an Oriental onion-domed tower but is marred by an out-of-character two-story porch probably added around 1910.

28 House

929 Hague Ave.

Louis Lockwood, 1900

Louis Lockwood is not nearly as well known in St. Paul as his contemporaries Cass Gilbert and Clarence Johnston, but he was a talented architect who occasionally liked to walk on the wild side. Here, he produced a striking design that grafts a fanciful Victorian-style porch with a conical roof onto the front of a fairly standard Colonial Revival house. Against all odds, the juxtaposition works. There's also a porte cochere to one side of the house, topped by an added-on sleeping porch.

POI B S. Edward Hall House N

996 Iglehart Ave.

1889

This small wood-frame house was the longtime home of a black barbershop owner and civic leader who played a key role in organizing the St. Paul Urban League.

29 Susan Welch House

785 Dayton Ave.

Clarence H. Johnston, 1894

The most monumental home in this part of St. Paul, presiding over its modest surroundings with an air of regal aplomb. Colossal Ionic columns rising from pedestals form a dignified temple front, behind which are double entrance doors and a graceful balcony with iron railings. Strong but simple detailing, including corner pilasters, reinforces the home's presence. The porte cochere on the west side of the house was originally balanced by a balustraded porch on the east side. Little is known about the house's original owner other than that she apparently did not wish to be upstaged by any of her neighbors.

Gideon Ives House

30 Gideon Ives House

625 Marshall Ave.

Thomas Holyoke, 1903

One of the few stone houses in this neighborhood, and a very quiet, refined example of Colonial Revival. The meticulously laid-up walls are of Mankato-Kasota limestone. The house was built for a lawyer but was apparently later used as the parsonage for Lutheran Church of the Redeemer, located a block to the north.

Susan Welch House

Lutheran Church of the Redeemer

31 Lutheran Church of the Redeemer

285 North Dale St.

Augustus Gauger, 1910 / addition, Slifer and Abrahamson, 1922 / addition, 1974

Augustus Gauger didn't design many churches—houses and commercial buildings were his métier—but here he showed he could do a Gothic Revival turn as well as the next fellow. Clad in rock-faced Mankato-Kasota limestone, the church has a square tower of the "crown" variety that culminates in a kingly array of sprockets and finials. The congregation was founded in 1890 and built this church for just $35,000, a tenth of what a 1974 addition cost.

Annotated Bibliography

Adams, John S., and Barbara J. VanDrasek. *Minneapolis–St. Paul: People, Place and Public Life*. Minneapolis: University of Minnesota Press, 1993. Written by two geographers, this book provides a useful overview of the growth and development of the Twin Cities.

Blodgett, Geoffrey. *Cass Gilbert: The Early Years*. St. Paul: Minnesota Historical Society Press, 2001. Much information about the early St. Paul career of the man who designed the Minnesota State Capitol and many other monuments.

Brooks, H. Allen. *The Prairie School: Frank Lloyd Wright and His Midwest Contemporaries*. 1972. Reprint, New York: Norton, 1976. Still the best survey of the Prairie School, with much information about its chief Minnesota practitioners, William Purcell and George Elmslie.

Castle, Henry A. *History of St. Paul and Vicinity: A Chronicle of Progress*. 3 vols. Chicago and New York: Lewis Publishing Co., 1912. An encyclopedic work that amply displays the biases of its era. But it's an enjoyable read (in spots) and offers much information not readily available elsewhere.

Christen, Barbara S., and Steven Flanders. *Cass Gilbert, Life and Work: Architect of the Public Domain*. New York: Norton, 2001. Includes a chapter on Gilbert's career in St. Paul.

Diers, John W., and Aaron Isaacs. *Twin Cities by Trolley: The Streetcar Era in Minneapolis and St. Paul*. Minneapolis: University of Minnesota Press, 2007. The fullest account available of the streetcar system that helped shape the Hill District and almost every other neighborhood in the Twin Cities.

Discover St. Paul: A Short History of Seven St. Paul Neighborhoods. St. Paul: Ramsey County Historical Society, 1979. Historical sketches illustrated with maps and photographs.

Empson, Donald L. *The Street Where You Live: A Guide to the Place Names of St. Paul*. Minneapolis: University of Minnesota Press, 2006. If you've ever wondered how St. Paul acquired so many unusual street names, you'll find the answers here.

Frame, Robert M. III. *James J. Hill's St. Paul: A Guide*. St. Paul: James J. Hill Reference Library, 1988. Identifies various St. Paul buildings associated with the fabled Empire Builder.

Gebhard, David, and Tom Martinson. *A Guide to the Architecture of Minnesota*. Minneapolis: University of Minnesota Press, 1977. Now badly dated, this remains the only comprehensive guide of its kind. The chapters on the Twin Cities omit many significant buildings, especially in St. Paul.

Hampl, Patricia, and Dave Page, eds. *The St. Paul Stories of F. Scott Fitzgerald*. St. Paul: Borealis Books, 2004. Some of Fitzgerald's most famous stories focused on his early years in St. Paul, and they're all here, collected for the first time in one volume. Hampl's introduction is superb.

Hennessy, William B. *Past and Present of St. Paul, Minnesota*. Chicago: S. J. Clarke Publishing Co., 1906. Another big subscription book, offering lots of secondhand information with a few good photographs.

Hess, Jeffrey A., and Paul Clifford Larson. *St. Paul Architecture: A History*. Minneapolis: University of Minnesota Press, 2006. The most thorough account of St. Paul's architectural history available. The chapter on Period Revival architecture is especially good.

Irish, Sharon. *Cass Gilbert, Architect: Modern Traditionalist.* New York: Monacelli Press, 1999. A biography of Minnesota's most famous architect.

Kenney, Dave. *Twin Cities Album: A Visual History.* St. Paul: Minnesota Historical Society Press, 2005. A nice array of photographs and other images that provide an overview of the history of Minneapolis and St. Paul. There's also an informative text.

Koeper, H. F. *Historic St. Paul Buildings.* St. Paul: City Planning Board, 1964. This booklet, published as the preservation movement was just getting under way, identified nearly 100 St. Paul buildings thought to be historically and architecturally significant. Alas, not all of them survived the 1960s.

Kudalis, Eric, ed. *100 Places Plus 1: An Unofficial Architectural Survey of Favorite Minnesota Sites.* Minneapolis: AIA Minnesota, 1996. Various essayists describe their favorite buildings and places in Minnesota.

Kunz, Virginia. *The Mississippi and St. Paul: A Short History of the City's 150-Year Love Affair with Its River.* St. Paul: Ramsey County Historical Society, 1987. A brief but informative look at how the Mississippi River shaped St. Paul's development and vice versa.

————. *St. Paul: Saga of an American City.* Woodland Hills, CA: Windsor Publications, 1977. A glossy "corporate history" that tends to plow familiar ground.

Larson, Paul Clifford. *Minnesota Architect: The Life and Work of Clarence H. Johnston.* Afton, MN: Afton Historical Society Press, 1996. A detailed study of Johnston, who designed numerous important buildings in St. Paul and at the University of Minnesota. Includes a complete catalog of his work.

Larson, Paul Clifford, with Susan Brown, eds. *The Spirit of H. H. Richardson on the Midland Prairies: Regional Transformations of an Architectural Style.* Minneapolis and Ames: University of Minnesota Art Museum and Iowa State University Press, 1988. A series of essays examining the influence, in the Twin Cities and elsewhere, of the great Boston architect Henry Hobson Richardson.

Lindley, John M. *Celebrate St. Paul: 150 Years of History.* Encino, CA: Cherbo Publishing Group, 2003. The latest history of St. Paul, profusely illustrated.

McAlester, Virginia, and Lee McAlester. *A Field Guide to American Houses.* New York: Alfred A. Knopf, 1984. Obviously this isn't a work about the Twin Cities, but it is a superb guidebook, with excellent drawings and photographs to help you identify the style of almost any kind of house.

Maccabee, Paul. *John Dillinger Slept Here: A Crooks' Tour of Crime and Corruption in St. Paul, 1920–1936.* St. Paul: Minnesota Historical Society Press, 1995. Everything you ever wanted to know about St. Paul's gangster era in the 1920s and 1930s. Includes excellent maps.

Martin, Judith, and Antony Goddard. *Past Choices/Present Landscapes: The Impact of Urban Renewal on the Twin Cities.* Minneapolis: Center for Urban and Regional Affairs, 1989. A straightforward account of how urban renewal dramatically altered St. Paul and Minneapolis.

Martin, Judith, and David Lanegran. *Where We Live: The Residential Districts of Minneapolis and Saint Paul.* Minneapolis: University of Minnesota Press, 1983. Lots of good information about neighborhoods in the Twin Cities.

Millett, Larry. *AIA Guide to the Twin Cities: The Essential Source on the Architecture of Minneapolis and St. Paul.* St. Paul: Minnesota Historical

Society Press, 2007. Includes chapters on Summit Avenue, the Hill District, and surrounding neighborhoods.

Millett, Larry (with photographs by Jerry Mathiason). *Twin Cities Then and Now*. St. Paul: Minnesota Historical Society Press, 1996. Historic photographs of more than 70 street scenes paired with new pictures taken from the same locations, including two from the Hill District.

Mulfinger, Dale. *The Architecture of Edwin Lundie*. St. Paul: Minnesota Historical Society Press, 1995. An overview of the work of Lundie, a master architect known for his romantic stone and wood houses, one of which is in the Hill District.

Murphy, Patricia, and Susan Granger. *Historic Sites Survey of Saint Paul and Ramsey County, 1980–1983: Final Report*. St. Paul: St. Paul Heritage Preservation Commission and Ramsey County Historical Society, 1983. A survey of significant architecture in St. Paul and Ramsey County. The report contains errors and omissions, but it's an invaluable reference document.

Newson, Thomas N. *Pen Sketches of St. Paul, Minnesota, and Biographical Sketches of Old Settlers, from the Earliest Settlement of the City, up to and including the Year 1857*. St. Paul: The Author, 1886. The title says it all. A big, quirky book that is usually interesting and in places downright amusing.

Nord, Mary Ann, comp. *The National Register of Historic Places in Minnesota*. St. Paul: Minnesota Historical Society Press, 2003. Lists every Minnesota building on the register.

Old Town Restorations, Inc. *Building the Future from Our Past: A Report on the Saint Paul Historic Hill District Planning Program*. St. Paul: Old Town Restorations, Inc., 1975. An excellent book that provided a blueprint for the Hill District's renaissance.

———. *Selby Avenue: Status of the Street*. St. Paul: Old Town Restorations, Inc., 1978. A planning guide devoted to one of the Hill District's most important streets.

Olson, Russell L. *The Electric Railways of Minnesota*. Hopkins: Minnesota Transportation Museum, 1977. Written by a trolley buff, this study describes in sometimes numbing detail the Twin Cities' late, great streetcar system.

Poppeliers, John C., S. Allen Chambers, Jr., and Nancy B. Schwartz. *What Style Is It? A Guide to American Architecture*. 1983. Rev. ed., Washington, DC: Preservation Press, ca. 2002. A useful guidebook that includes photographs, drawings, a glossary of terms, and a good bibliography.

Prairie School Architecture in Minnesota, Iowa, Wisconsin. St. Paul: Minnesota Museum of Art, 1982. Six essays on Prairie School architecture, lavishly illustrated with photographs and drawings.

Pyle, J. G., ed. *Picturesque St. Paul*. St. Paul: Northwestern Photo Co., 1888. Great photographs of old-time St. Paul, assembled by the man who wrote the first biography of James J. Hill.

Richter, Bonnie, ed. *Saint Paul Omnibus: Images of the Changing City*. St. Paul: Old Town Restorations, Inc., 1979. A nice booklet that explores the city's architectural history.

Sandeen, Ernest. *St. Paul's Historic Summit Avenue*. 1978. Minneapolis: University of Minnesota Press, 2004. Although Sandeen's architectural judgments are a bit eccentric, this book is a delight to read and remains the best guide to St. Paul's most famous thoroughfare. Includes a catalog of houses on the avenue.

Schmid, Calvin F. *Social Saga of Two Cities: An Ecological and Statistical Study of Social Trends in Minneapolis and St. Paul.* Minneapolis: Council of Social Agencies, Bureau of Social Research, 1937. Conceived as a Depression-era project, this is one of the most informative books ever written about the Twin Cities. Especially valuable are the superb maps and charts.

Taylor, David Vassar, and Paul Clifford Larson. *Cap Wigington: An Architectural Legacy in Ice and Stone.* St. Paul: Minnesota Historical Society Press, 2001. A good account of the life and work of St. Paul's first black architect.

Vincent, Jeanne Anne. *St. Paul Architecture, 1848–1906.* Master's thesis, University of Minnesota, 1944. An early study of St. Paul's historic architecture. Includes many photographs.

Warner, George E., and Charles M. Foote, comps. *History of Ramsey County and the City of St. Paul, including the Explorers and Pioneers of Minnesota, by Edward D. Neill, and Outlines of the History of Minnesota, by J. Fletcher Williams.* Minneapolis: North Star Publishing Co., 1881. A useful compendium, even if the title seems nearly as long as the book.

Williams, J. Fletcher. *A History of the City of Saint Paul to 1875.* 1887. St. Paul: Minnesota Historical Society, 1983. A good "snack" book, filled with colorful stories of early St. Paul.

Wingerd, Mary Lethert. *Claiming the City: Politics, Faith, and the Power of Place in St. Paul.* Ithaca, NY: Cornell University Press, 2001. One of the best books ever written about St. Paul. It offers a convincing explanation for why St. Paul is in many ways so different from Minneapolis.

Young, Biloine Whiting, and David Lanegran. *Grand Avenue: The Renaissance of an Urban Street.* St. Cloud, MN: North Star Press, 1996. A rather informal book that explains how the once seedy avenue came back to life as St. Paul's most upscale shopping venue.

Index

Every building and site described in the Guide is listed as a primary entry in the index, both by previous and current names. Building and street names beginning with "North," "South," "East," or "West" are inverted and alphabetized under the keyword part of the street name (e.g., "North St. Albans" is alphabetized as "St. Albans St. North"). Building and street names beginning with numbers are alphabetized as if spelled out. The names of people, firms, organizations, and government offices involved in creating the works listed in the Guide appear in Upper and Lower Case Small Caps. Unless otherwise indicated, they are architects, associated artists, or builders. Names of geographic areas appear in **boldface italic**. A page reference in **boldface** indicates a photograph of the building, area, or other work.

The following abbreviations appear in the index:

Amer.	American	Condos.	Condominiums	Mpls.	Minneapolis
Assn.	Association	Corp.	Corporation	Natl.	National
Assocs.	Associates	Ct.	Court	Pkwy.	Parkway
Apts.	Apartments	Dept.	Department	St.	Street
Bldg.	Building	H.S.	High School	Univ.	University
Bros.	Brothers	Intl.	International		
Co.	Company	MN	Minnesota		

Picture Credits

AIA Guide to St. Paul's Summit Avenue and Hill District was designed by Cathy Spengler Design, Minneapolis. Typesetting by Allan Johnson, Phoenix Type, Appleton, Minnesota. Printed by Friesens, Altona, Manitoba.